MEET ME IN
BUENOS AIRES

MEET ME IN
BUENOS AIRES

A Memoir

Marlene Hobsbawm

**MUSWELL
PRESS**

First published by Muswell Press in 2019

Typeset by M Rules

Printed and bound by CPI Group (UK) Ltd, Croydon CR0 4YY.

ISBN: 9781999313579

Muswell Press
London
N6 5HQ
www.muswell-press.co.uk

For the joyful grandchildren:
Roman, Anoushka, Wolfgang, Milo, Eve,
Rachael and Maxim.

Contents

Prologue

Becoming a singleton after fifty years of marriage was an adventure of its own. And starting the endeavour of writing a memoir at eighty-five was quite optimistic, as my vocabulary and memory are diminishing.

I didn't set out to write a memoir: it was a project that unfolded slowly. Once the Cambridge historian Sir Richard Evans expressed his interest in writing my husband Eric's biography, I naturally became very involved. This seven-year undertaking stirred up memories of my own life – from times before, with and after Eric. Once I began, I found myself compelled to continue, but above all, I wanted my grandchildren to know about my life.

Not being a historian, I was more interested in remembering life from another angle – piecing together a record of family, friendship, travel and an unwavering love between two unlikely individuals.

Introduction

The Hobsbawms – Eric and Marlene – always seemed to me an example of a perfect couple, mutually devoted and at the same time welcoming friends to their house with extraordinary generosity. Invitations to dinners came regularly, to Sunday lunches, to visit them in their cottage in Wales, to celebrate at memorable parties. With Marlene and Eric you always enjoyed yourselves – good talk, good jokes, good arguments, good friends, good food, good wine. And Marlene was cook and organiser, while also teaching music, raising the children and dealing with every sort of practical problem thrown up by family life and marriage to a hard-working and celebrated husband.

I knew Eric by reputation when I was an undergraduate at Cambridge, and my friend Neal Ascherson was taught by him and spoke of him with admiration. While researching my first book in the early 1970s, I therefore consulted Eric on some historical points. My subject was Mary Wollstonecraft, who proclaimed the rights of women in the 1790s, and my impression was that he was not exactly a feminist, while being more kind and helpful in his response than I could have hoped, as indeed he was whenever I asked for advice or help. He also wrote the occasional review for me when I worked on the *New Statesman* in the mid-seventies, and this was when I went to their house in Hampstead for the first time and met Marlene. I thought she was amazing – and we formed a friendship that has strengthened ever since: forty-five years, I make it.

I realise now how little I knew of her early life, although we were almost the same age and both had continental origins – I French, she Viennese. I understood she had been brought to England as a small child when her father, a successful businessman, saw how dangerous Hitler was. I once asked her about learning a second language and she gave me a charming account of how she had refused to speak a word of English for a long time – I suppose it was a form of protest at being uprooted – but that one day her mother, listening outside the room where she was playing alone, heard her addressing her dolls in perfectly good English. The stubborn, clever child predicted the versatile and charming woman.

Reading her memoir I realise that she and I shared the experience of being sent off to boarding schools we did not always like – she ran away, I fell ill – and that as young women we were both exploring Paris at about the same time, studying French history, reading Gide and Colette, entranced by *Les Enfants du Paradis*, Prévert, Charles Trenet, and the streets, bridges, parks and paintings in the galleries.

We both also went through the then almost obliga-tory ritual for young women of learning secretarial skills. After that she, with immense dash, took herself to Italy and found jobs in Rome and Capri, lived a life of utmost sophistication, and moved on to work in the Congo for a year. Adventurous, brave and loyal, she made friends wherever she went, and kept them.

She was twenty-nine when she met and married Eric. He was already known as a scholar, teacher and historian whose books became instant classics, and was greatly in demand as a speaker all over the world. Marlene often travelled with him while also bringing up their son and daughter and establishing a home life that gave him time and space to work. 'In my head I'm a continental woman,' she writes: I think this means she knows how to combine domestic and intellectual life and make it look easy.

But it is not easy. Marlene gave Eric the support he needed to achieve greatness while always remaining a strong and decisive person in her own right. In effect, she taught him by her strength to respect feminism. Her memoir, starting from the sadness of exile and war in childhood, reveals her on every page as enterprising, courageous and warm-hearted – and is a delight to read.

Claire Tomalin
July 2019

Chapter 1
Vienna Beginnings

I was born in Vienna in 1932, the third and youngest child of Louise (Lilly) and Theodore (Theo) Schwarz. My older brothers were Victor Hugo (Vicky), who was five years old and Walter, two years old. On the whole, Mother brought us up mostly as *die Kinder* – the children – and I liked being lumped together like this even when not keeping up. I felt safe and happy. We had a nanny and a maid, and lived in the leafy suburb of Döbling.

My father, a middle child of ten children, came from Innsbruck. He was lively and not the type to stay put in the Tyrol. As a young man he enterprisingly got himself a job in the luxury hotel business in Paris, where he completely fell for the city, the French, and the cosmopolitan life around him. Later on, he became a businessman in the textile industry. He must have had a flair for it, as we lived well. I believe he had a good reputation and he enjoyed his work, especially travelling and making contacts all over Europe. He spoke several languages and was very interested in politics. Mother had to save all the English newspapers for him when he went away on his business trips. His mother, Grandma Rosa, was our only living grandparent. She regularly came to visit us in Vienna and we had holidays in her house in Igls, up in the hills above Innsbruck. She had a reputation for being difficult, but my mother liked and respected her.

My mother Lilly was born in Vienna, the youngest of five, and was such a late arrival that her siblings were already aged eighteen, seventeen, sixteen, and eleven. Her nearest sister Emmy was responsible for most of her upbringing. Mother remembered a school friend saying, 'You don't have to do what she says – she is only your sister.' Lilly did not have a career and was twenty-one when she married my father. Their roles were pretty clear: Father was the teacher and Mother the pupil. Jumping ahead twenty-five years, my own marriage followed a not entirely dissimilar pattern.

My nursery school was located in the basement of our building, which must have felt cosy, and it was run by my mother's niece. I remember going down long steps willingly and coming back up again. I was about three years old.

During this time, which seems like idyllic family life, my parents had many anxieties, as they were planning to leave Austria for good. My father believed the things that Adolf Hitler was saying in his speeches and he realised the dangers so close in Germany, unlike many of our Viennese friends and family, who never believed Hitler would carry out his plans. My brothers were being prepared for this dramatic change, especially my elder brother Vicky. But nothing was said to me. I was considered too young and was to be protected. My mother and brothers were already having English lessons. My brother

Walter (who became a journalist) has written his own memoir *The Ideal Occupation*[1], which depicts this early part of our lives extremely well and in more detail.

---

1   Walter Schwarz, The Ideal Occupation (Brighton: Revel Barker Publishing, 2011), pp. 6–30.

Chapter 2

Wartime Children: The Émigré Child and my Education

We arrived in London as émigrés when I was five. Our home was a flat in a large mansion block in Hammersmith. During the day, the dark, empty garages in the basement were where the children of the flats used to play, and we all joined them. One day, during that horrible game of hide-and-seek (while both my protective brothers were at school), I became very scared when it was my turn to find the other children. Even though I had known so well in advance that I couldn't find them on my own, I just couldn't say it and began sobbing instead. That rather traumatic experience stayed with me, and I got into the habit of often preparing and forestalling to stave off disaster. 'Marlene, why are you worrying about that *now*?' people say. The answer would be: I believe in the power of worry. It works.

I was sent to a Froebel nursery school[2] and refused to

---

2   Friedrich Froebel (1782–1852) established the first kindergartens (and coined the term), using a play-based learning system.

speak for the whole year I was there. The teachers said I seemed settled and spent my time mainly playing in the sandpit. But I had become a self-imposed mute. Maybe it was a fear of not speaking English well enough (I think I was confused about being a German-speaking child at home), or it could have been stubbornness, or maybe I was upset at not being a proper English girl like the others. Being unprepared meant everything came as a shock, and I think it was the beginning of the University of Life for me.

In 1938, a year later, we left London to live in Manchester, where I was enrolled in the junior school of Manchester High School for Girls. However, with the outbreak of war in 1939, all children were evacuated; Vicky was sent to Blackpool and Walter and I to Uttoxeter in Staffordshire. I can see the huge room full of children sitting on the floor with gas-mask cases and belongings. We were supposed to go to our families in pairs, and I was expecting to be with Walter, when suddenly a lady announced that there was a family who would only take one child and 'would anybody volunteer'. My heart sank because I knew my brother Walter's hand would shoot up, and indeed it did. I don't remember any goodbye. And so we were all dispersed. Only Mother and Father were together.

My foster family lived in a small, modest house and another child my age also lodged there. My recollection is that everything seemed brown, both inside and out. I began to lie like a trooper, telling them all sorts of imaginary tales about my real family in Manchester. I invented a baby brother and told them a lot about 'him'. Even though I knew my parents were coming to visit very soon, when I would be unmasked to one and all, I still couldn't stop. 'Should I get nappies?' asked my foster mother, 'Oh yes,' I said, 'Definitely.' Later my mother told me she just couldn't make me out, and I could not explain. Life was incomprehensible to me. I found that praying did no good whatsoever, but instead my rosier fantasies consoled me. And they still do, but now I keep them to myself. Psychology must have been unknown to my folks at that time, despite us being a typical Freudian nuclear family from Vienna.

We could attend a nearby school on alternate days to the local children. I can remember an open shelter outside, but of the inside I remember nothing. I was in a trance. Walter went to his foster family at the end of the same village but we never coincided. One day, on my own, I walked to the large mansion he was staying in (with a Rolls-Royce in the garage) and rang the bell. A servant came to the gate with a very big dog and I asked to speak to my brother. I was told to wait right there. Walter soon appeared and said, 'What do you want?' and I was suddenly struck dumb, answering, 'I don't know.' In my head I had prepared to ask, 'Tell me again exactly why we are here.' He just replied, 'If you don't want anything I will continue what I was doing,' or something along those lines.

Luckily we were not evacuated for long. There was a military miscalculation (not unknown in wartime) and when the Blitz started in earnest – when the bombs really fell – we were all back again in our own homes in the big cities, ready targets for the whistling bombs.

But the Blitz was a good time for me because of the nightlife in the bunks in our well-kitted-out cellar. We were all of us together, and that is the only thing I wanted. We ate delicious food that Mother had prepared during the day and it all seemed very jolly to me, not to mention my lovely new red boiler-jumpsuit (only to be worn during air raids). The long raids provided another advantage. Children under a certain age, like me, did not have to go to school the following day and I spent my time with the women in the house: my mother, our Irish cleaner and one of my father's sisters, Tante Hedi, who used to shriek, 'The veesling bombs!' when she heard a noise. I also played with some of the children of the large Irish family across the road. But I knew my mother was worried about me. She wanted the best for me and so did my father. One of the children in our continental circle of friends, an only child of about ten called George, was apparently happily settled in an English Quaker boarding school in Wigton, Cumberland. It had a good reputation and was known as Brookfield.

Alas, my parents, thinking that an English boarding school was synonymous with the best in life and where I would make many English friends, thought it would be a good idea for me. But it was the worst idea ever.

I was nine when I was sent to the Friends' School, Brookfield. It must have been around this time that I began to switch off from even trying to understand what was going on in my world, which had once again been turned upside down. What the heck was WAR, anyway? Had there been television I probably would have fared better. None of it made sense to me. It was beyond me to figure it out. I turned myself from out to in and became a very un-inquisitive child. I continued with my vague notion that grown-up minds are different and I had better think for myself.

The boarding school was situated in the beautiful Cumbrian countryside and I remember lovely long walks on Sunday, to and from church. But I was very unhappy to be there in spite of it being an interesting school. All letters home had to be shown to our teachers first. But during the holidays I told my parents about desperately wanting to leave and come home. My father said he would find an alternative and meanwhile I should give some letters to the day children to post for me. He sent me stamps, which I managed to hide safely, so I could write freely – I can see one of my letters now: *I carn't bare it* (sic). And father wrote back to be patient, but I wasn't.

I say I was 'unhappy', but of course children carry on with their lives in unhappiness. I have some letters of mine, which seem quite typical of any boarding-school girl writing home about her activities and most likely I stood in the queue for my skipping-rope turn just like everyone else. But then came the drama.

Towards the end of my second year at Brookfield, I ran away. Not only that, but my worst crime was that I went with a much younger girl! We got very far, reaching the train station, when they grabbed us. In any case the strategy I had in my head would have been doomed: it was to get off the train at any station and ask the way to the nearest police station. I knew my address in Manchester and was convinced that we would be helped – 'That is surely what policemen are for!' I had prepared to say to the police that if they helped me get home, my parents would definitely reimburse the fare. What panic there must have been at the school had we succeeded even a bit. There was an uproar and my parents were immediately summoned; finally they grasped my situation. I think a dog or a cat might have made a better fist of getting back home than I did.

Running away from boarding school brought about

the end of my dramas. I returned to the junior school of Manchester High School for Girls as before. My mother later told me that once I was back there and wearing the familiar red-checked dress and panama hat, and living at home, they seemed to have no more trouble with me. Maybe all my difficulties had finally been expelled. I sometimes think my generation of émigré children, who actually lived through this experience, felt better in some ways than the next generation, who could only wonder at the relayed stories of another past in another country. Some parents didn't want to talk about the past at all. My brother Walter, on the other hand, always rejoiced and felt blessed and lucky about being in England, and had nothing but praise for the foresight of our dad, who had the wisdom to get us away in comfort and ease when it was still possible to do so.

Vicky was ten when he came to England, and integrating was different for him. He must have had much deeper memories of Austria than Walter or me. He had the sunniest disposition and was used to being adored by his teachers in Vienna. He and Walter were sent to Colet Court Preparatory School for St Paul's in Hammersmith, and I sometimes imagine how he might have felt on his first day there in the playground. '*WHAT did you say your name was? SCHWARZ?!*' All conjecture on my part, but maybe around that time a tiny seed was sown which grew with his desire to be like an Englishman and above all, a gentleman. When he became an adult he decided to change his name to Victor Black (by deed poll), as when applying for jobs he was advised against a German name.

Chapter 3

Secondary School: Teens and Young Adults at Home

I am writing this story of our teenage years now in my ninth decade and as the proud grandmother of five grandchildren who are now around the same age as Vicky, Walter and I were then. It's difficult to compare the lives of these sophisticated Londoners who spend their time on smartphones and other screens, and are connected to the adult world 24/7, with us provincial children in wartime, living at half the pace. I can only hope for their future in a world more dangerous even than ours. Back to 1943, we are still at war and I am eleven, with a Lancashire accent. I went through to the senior school and at sixteen I passed my School Certificate (now GCSE). I can't honestly say I remember any particularly inspiring teachers or even any subjects with enormous enthusiasm but I suppose 'literature' as it was then called would be the strongest candidate. But even so I came away knowing no poetry or familiar books, except *Silas Marner*, which was permanently on the syllabus. I loathed more than anything in the world having to play hockey in the mud on Thursdays. I considered it barbaric. In the freezing cold our legs turned red, blue or purple. But a school medical found that I had a congenital heart murmur (hurray!) and so mercifully I was released from that immediately. My friends were very jealous.

My best friend was Leila Yael, who was the cleverest girl in the school, and although she eventually moved to Argentina, we have remained lifelong friends. Both of us named our first-born babies Andy. I was never short of friends but having two handsome brothers (who many girls already liked the look of) might have a part in this. Much later on, in my twenties, I was closer to Leila's sister Yvonne, who lived in Europe. Now as grannies, we all three correspond and meet, and any differences are trivial.

My brothers, who had been to 'South' prep school, were now already at Manchester Grammar School, which was not very far away from our Manchester High School for Girls. I think the interaction of the two schools and their pupils was similar to today. But maybe more money was spent, as I remember in addition to school concerts and sports, proper dances were also organised. I looked forward to them with both trepidation and anticipation. Again, having two brothers was a great advantage. I think one of Walter's friends had a crush on me, but I liked a quite different boy. In any case, we were all totally preoccupied with the impression we ourselves were making. Some children were already dating, and the girls would ask each other, 'Did you go all the way?'

Both my brothers were very good at school. Vicky was again popular with teachers and with classmates, and his glory was being the excellent goalkeeper of the school football team. He was eventually offered a place at Trinity College Dublin. For Vicky, having a good time was a high priority. He believed in it seriously and pursued it to make it happen —sometimes it felt like he was curating fun. Maybe this comes from the experience of being taken away from the glorious life that he knew in Vienna.

Walter was the family's scholar and one of those rare children who knew what he wanted to be when grown up: a journalist. He managed to finish his School Certificate exams with half a year to spare and later, after obtaining his Higher School Certificate (A levels), he won an Exhibition to Queen's College, Oxford. Mother's Viennese dreams about English education had indeed come true. She brought it up during one of our last conversations when she was already very frail.

School is all very well, but it is at home, within the family, that children spend so much of their lives and do most of their growing up. What sort of family were we? We were assimilated into British society and did not observe Jewish religious customs, but we were also consciously Jewish. We kept up our German-Viennese language and culture and at the same time fully absorbed all that we liked or disliked about England. Assimilation is usually easier for the children than the parents, and so it was with us: the fact that our Vic was the goalie for the Manchester Grammar School football team completely passed my father by, until one day he suddenly found himself a hero amongst his business colleagues over lunch.

We lived in Moorfield Road, West Didsbury and, after our initial short-lived evacuation, remained there throughout the war until 1953, when we all felt that London was the place to be. The family then moved into a three-storey house in Golders Green, which agreeably backed on to Golders Hill Park.

I think the atmosphere of our household was jolly and united. Passionately hating Hitler played a part in that. Vic, being the eldest child and with the sunniest nature, had, I think, the most admiration from our parents. Mother's favourite was Walter, as she couldn't resist his dreaminess and his earnestness. I was Daddy's girl, no mistake about that. There was rivalry between the boys, who were very different. Sometimes Vicky (who could make me do *anything*) and I ganged up on Walter. In turn and with ease, both boys cheated me with the household chores, and I was often teased. The tension between my brothers remained through their adult lives; they were just too different, but became most devoted fathers themselves. Mother's love was practical and father's sentimental. Mother usually understood my struggles, whatever they were, and always helped me. There was solidarity between us; we were a little team of our own, though I wish she had not been so successful at instilling her 'work before play' ethic in me. She was happy when I was, but I had to be useful too and pull my weight.

She was absolutely not a feminist. Her own upbringing had been too traditional. Boys' education was more important. If you wore trousers, you counted double. It didn't really harm me, apart from my education, of course, or rather my lack of it. Eric never quite managed to forgive her for that. When I wanted to give up Latin, it seemed OK by my parents. But now, seventy years later, I find myself the only person in my choir who can't sing in Latin. Luckily all the *Agnus Deis, Glorias, Jubilates, Hosannas in*

Excelsises, Hallelujahs and Miseres can carry one along for pages and pages.

Without television, the wireless was the glue in our lives. We of course followed the news intensely. During the war Father had pinned up a large map with little flags marking the progress and defeats of the Allied troops every day. We loved the BBC, and the beautiful spoken language that came from it. I remember a weekly radio programme, *Monday Night at Eight*, which we regularly listened to as a family. This show consisted of interviews with all types of people, a detective play, *Dr Morelle*, a 'Puzzle Corner' and a 'Deliberate Mistake.' I think all England listened, and so the whole country talked and joked about the same people.

As well as the wireless, at home we had books and the gramophone. We also went to the cinema. When later I was allowed to go on my own (what bliss) I saw *Lassie Come Home* four times. Films were quite different then: the normalities shown revolved around the wholesome family. For example, a couple could not be shown in a bed together unless they were married. And there were no gay people.

Father, from the Tyrol, was an organiser of excursions; what could be better than the Peak District on our doorstep. It felt as if we visited everywhere. We also went on holidays to North Wales, as father was keen on climbing. I climbed up Cader Idris, but went up Snowdon by train. We had a family whistle that was often used – and needed – to keep us together. We also had many holidays in the beautiful Lake District, especially Derwentwater near Keswick.

There was always a large circle of émigré and refugee friends whom we saw regularly. My father was considered a bit of a leader, or more respected because he was better informed. Some were frightened of rumours that Jews were going to be repatriated or such nonsense. My parents became bosom friends with Lilly and Ernst Stiglitz, also from Austria, and very cultured. They were an inseparable couple who had no children and loved spending time with us. They lived about twenty minutes' walk away and every single Sunday they either came to us or we went to them. Such was our cosy and predictable life. We had an allot-ment not far away, by the River Mersey. All of us émigrés were 'Digging for Victory' with gusto, even though we didn't know much about gardening.

Father was a gregarious man and made new friends easily, including many English ones. My parents knew a wide circle of people, including the historian A. J. P. Taylor, who also lived in Manchester then. My mother was a good housekeeper and produced lovely party food despite the shortages and the rationing. Our house was usually full of people, friends and also many relatives; some from London came for a respite from the bombing there. They also stayed for longer periods with us, like semi-lodgers, and had to bring their ration books.

Our status in England was as 'enemy aliens'. Father should at this point have been sent to the Isle of Man to be interned with many others, but a medical report came back positive for diabetes, so he stayed at home. He was not diabetic; it must have been a urine sample that got mixed up. We were safe but also had to be careful. There was an incident when Vic had left a tiny slit in the blackout curtains in his room and because of this we were reported, then inspected. But luckily it all ended with a smile at a schoolboy's slapdash oversight. Father, by the way, who was politically mostly on the right, idolised Churchill, who was his hero. It was common to support him at the time, as Eric notes in his biography, 'Churchill was associated with heroism.'

Mother was a good employer and usually had help with the housework from girls who were devoted to her. It wasn't a special skill, but her genuine interest and respect for every human being disarmed them. They came mainly from Ireland.

I didn't know until much later in life about my father's infidelity. Some of it only amounted to him flirting with nieces quite openly. But he had a French girlfriend who lived in Switzerland. The business trips must have made it easy for him, but onerous for Mother. I think she took it in her stride and, for all I know, tried to make it fit with her un-feminist views that 'men just are like that'.

When the war was finally over, it seemed obvious that the Victory Day party in 1945 would be held at our home. My father wanted us to wear Austrian dress, me in a dirndl (oh dear), in order to emphasise our gratitude to England, and I obliged.

Classical music played a huge part in our lives, which was the same in both cultures. Mother had a good soprano voice and loved opera best of all. When opera companies came on tour, we often went. My first opera was *The Bartered Bride* by Smetana. We were regularly taken to the Hallé Orchestra concerts, possibly every week, especially when Sir John Barbirolli himself conducted. This was our Manchester orchestra and we were by now loyal Mancunians. There was a baby grand piano at home and we children all had piano lessons. Walter was the most passionate about music, and from time to time he turned our sitting room – as best he could – into a concert stage. His imaginary orchestra always had their same places – strings by the fireplace, woodwind near the door, and so on. He then proceeded to elaborately conduct from the score of a Beethoven symphony, which he also had playing loudly on the gramophone.

Walter also learned to play the recorder rather well, and had a school friend, Peter Noble, with whom he played duets at home. That was my first introduction to this lovely instrument, which many years later became my own.

Growing older, we were slowly gearing up to leave school and the nest, and thinking about our futures. Walter was called up for his military service after his time at Oxford and was sent to Malaya. Wherever he went, his thoughts were mainly about writing it down on paper in preparation for becoming a journalist. He did this when writing home to us as well. But I recall Mother and I crying our eyes out when we had taken him to Liverpool to board the gigantic steamer for Malaya and war. Walter did indeed become a very well-known journalist and spent his life being a foreign correspondent for the *Guardian* news-paper in Nigeria, Israel, India and France, all written about in his entertaining memoir. He married a woman named Dorothy Morgan and they had five children together: Habie, Tanya, Ben, Zoe and Zac.

Our Vic's story is different. He not only believed in FUN, he engineered it. Goodness knows where his gift for pleasure sprang from in a cautious, earnest émigré family like ours. When I was about fifteen, I remember a weekend when Vic invited the entire chorus of the D'Oyly Carte Opera, who were on tour in Manchester, to a party at our house. My parents were away on a trip and Walter was also away. I was quite used to Vic's girlfriends being very kind to me and I liked their company, but this party, I felt, was boring, because lots of them went to bed early: I was a late developer and pretty naïve about sexual matters, let alone orgies. Different from some of today's savvy girls. When our parents returned, the house was all tidied up, the laundry done, and everything was in immaculate condition, except one of mum's devoted cleaners was in tears, repeating hysterically 'Only for you, Mrs Schwarz, I stayed in this house, only for you.'

Hedonism got seriously out of control at Trinity College in Dublin, where Vic only stayed one term as he had spent all the money that Father had given him for his three years of study. How foolish was Father – and Vic. All spent on women; the money was gone. He enjoyed being a chivalrous gentleman with his friends. His heart, however, was in politics and he did support work for his local Conservative association and was particularly interested in helping young offenders. He was excellent at this. He later joined and then took over Father's textile business, at which he was very good. I think it was also helpful for Father who, tragically, was hatching Parkinson's disease. The responsibility both changed and suited Vic. And years later, when our father died and mother was alone, he looked after her financial affairs and also continued his gallant ways, such as collecting her from the airport, and making her feel she still had a man to lean on. It gave her such enormous reassurance and pleasure.

Vic came into his own as a family man with the pride and pleasure he took in each and every one. With his wife Oonagh and four children (Emily, Isobel, Charlotte and Humphrey), there was plenty to report, and the news always seemed to be something marvellous; I know he helped with homework and essays because once he mentioned triumphantly on the phone, 'We got an A.' He took his family to Austria for holidays when he could, much more than the rest of us. He hankered after mountains, lakes and scenery, probably liked speaking German and could taste and introduce to his family P*ovidla tascherln* (cheese dumplings), *Kaiserschmarrn* (a fluffy shredded pancake) and *Palatschinken* (jam pancakes) – favourite desserts from early childhood.

Chapter 4
A Student in Paris

I am now sixteen. Father had always talked to me about 'abroad' and I must have got my itch to travel from him. I already loved Paris before I ever went and remember he had taught me the song from the opera *Manon*, which he loved: '*Nous irons à Paris tous les deux.*' After leaving school at sixteen (going on seventeen), I went to Paris to learn French. As this was 1948, I think I might have been one of the first ever *au pair* girls.

My first charge was four-year-old Irène and we had heaps of fun together every day, the highlight being eating pain au chocolat at four o'clock in the Jardins du Trocadéro. I loved her, but not the family, who called me 'Mademoiselle' all the year I was there, never Marlene. They were rich; we lived in a grand penthouse in the Avenue Kléber, but we didn't really click. Looking back, I think they were my first 'nouveaux riches' acquaintances, and I didn't play my cards right at all. When feeling lonely, I would sometimes chat with the cook in the kitchen, which was very frowned upon.

I had enrolled in the two-year course at the Alliance

Francaise to study the French language in the first year and French literature in the second. The first year was all in the Boulevard Raspail and in the second year the course tied up with the Sorbonne University, where many lectures and events were held. At seventeen, and with a bounce, some education began at long last. I was captivated. One of my teachers in the first year, who liked me, was expecting a baby and asked me to commit to being her au pair in my second year, which I did. It was an important and very wise decision. Nadia turned out to be as interested in my French education as I was. I became a student completely engrossed in my studies and the culture around them. She treated me as her daughter.

My duties with the baby were mostly only until lunchtime, and much of that was going to Parc Monceau and reading while he slept. Baby Michel was an absolute angel, and I adored him. If I were an artist I would be able to draw his smile this very day, sixty-eight years since I saw it. I can always conjure him up.

The Hugons lived in the Rue de Rome and Nadia's husband Bernard, who worked in Lille, only came home at weekends. They then liked to be together at home, so I was not expected to do much babysitting even at weekends. I was free to study, go to my classes and wander endlessly around the city. I had plenty of time for gallivanting with my friends and getting glimpses of the so-talked-about Paris by night. Every weekday I took the bus to Boulevard Raspail, not tiring of looking at Île de la Cité, The Louvre, the contours of Notre Dame, the river Seine and its bridges: Pont St Michel, Pont Neuf and Pont des Arts.

The old-fashioned Alliance Française was a serious place with a very good ambience. Most of us were foreigners (several Scandinavians) and we were not all grown up. We were like A-level schoolchildren, but not at home.

Our reading list was not all ancient or difficult. Certainly Racine had to be there, *Andromaque* and *Phèdre*, and Molière's *Le Misanthrope*, but, in an enlightened way, the syllabus concentrated on more contemporary plays like Anouilh's *Antigone* so that we could engage with criticism on a controversial work and further debate among ourselves. It was wonderful to study the plays people were talking about in cafés. Being in touch seemed very important to Parisians and I wanted to be too. We then went on to study Marcel Pagnol's *César, Fanny* and *Marius,* all of which we had to read aloud in class in a *Provençal accent*! Really, they wanted the students to learn about the Midi region and get the *feel* of it. The Alliance Française's fresh approach to education was quite unique, unusual and certainly new.

A bunch of us took a trip down to Cannes and for a lark we flagged cars, shouting, '*Sales capitalistes!*' at the tops of our voices. We considered ourselves left wing, though what we knew about politics that sunny day could fit on a postage stamp. We also sang together; our favourites were Edith Piaf and Charles Trenet, and the favourite of all was Yves Montand singing 'Les feuilles mortes' by Jacques Prévert. I sent a letter to Walter full of excitement that I was now on a level to discuss literature and other issues with him. It was meant to impress him with my new sophistication in general. I look at the envelope and smile.

My own personal reading continued with two brilliant tomes of André Gide's journals which I read in daily instalments. For sheer delight and relaxation, there was Colette – the *Claudine* series, and the *Cheri* books and *Gigi*, among others. I was also inspired by Simone de Beauvoir and wanted to copy her self-contained studious ways of being alone in public places. With Sartre, I only liked the existential bit that focused on the absurdity of existence. But at the same time, I gravitated more strongly towards the mood and romance of the city. I was 17 and it was springtime in Paris. I remember the enchantment and feeling overwhelmed by it all. How could one be serious about politics anyway, when you have just seen the film *Les Enfants du Paradis* for the first time. It remains a timeless romantic epic and has since been voted the best French film of all time.

Chapter 5

Working in London and Secretarial College

I came home to England with good French under my belt but no obvious employable talents, and I was nineteen. Mum and I made the next decisions and I enrolled at the Marlborough Gate Secretarial College in the Bayswater Road London for a year. The skills I learned there led to my first ever full-time paid job.

Who would have thought an unbeliever like myself would be thrust headlong into the ecclesiastical world, even though I had always loved singing Christian hymns? I enjoy some Christian verse, and I have found it useful to have a copy of *Songs of Praise* as a reference book at hand. In my new job I had become in charge of the subscription and distribution of a Church of England periodical called *The Pulpit Monthly*.

Each issue contained four ready-made articles and ideas to inspire clergymen for their Sunday sermons. Sometimes they panicked when it failed to arrive, as they hadn't yet thought of anything to say. It seemed that I corresponded with all the parish priests, vicars, chaplains, ministers, pastors and rectors of England. They depended on me. They were invariably charming, and sent kind words and little presents too, as though I had written the sermons myself. The office was in the city, right next to St Paul's Cathedral, where I sometimes spent some of my lunchtime, and my lodgings were in Putney, in a beautiful flat overlooking the Thames.

I was consulted by my landlady about which applicant should occupy the second bedroom in her flat. The choice was between three: a Swedish girl, which sounded too unfamiliar, a French boy, which would be useless, as there was only one bathroom, and an Italian girl. I chose her, not knowing she would alter the course of my life. Mariella de Sarzana and I got on very well. We became friends, I invited her to come home to spend Christmas with us, and in the summer, during my holidays, I was invited to visit her in Rome. Now in my early twenties, I went all the way by train, a long journey through France and Switzerland. At the Stazione Termini in Rome, Mariella was waiting for me.

The very first sentence she excitedly and breathlessly said was, 'I need to go to Capri tomorrow and see some people, and find Kirk Douglas. Will you come with me, pleeese?' Of course I said yes. Mariella knew everyone. Gracie Fields was there and I remember meeting her. Mariella was besotted with American films, and was making contacts to get herself, by hook or by crook, to Hollywood, which she eventually did. In Capri we found Kirk Douglas and travelled back to Rome with him – he flirting and playing footsy under the table with both of us.

The island of Capri is surely one of the most beautiful

in the world. The higher part is Anacapri, with the villa of San Michele, which the doctor and author Axel Munthe had built at the turn of the century. It is in grandiose, palatial style amidst huge and flamboyant flora, and has its own museum.

The lower part of the island, which descends all the way down to the sea, is a holiday resort with taste: grand hotels with pools, and smaller ones too. There were luxury shops and people running around in Emilio Pucci's 'palazzo pants'. At the end, just off the coast, are situated those two majestic landmark rocks surrounded by sky and sea blues, but not blues I had ever seen before. I was overcome by the colours and felt my life had only been in black and white until that day. It was in part because of this visit that I fell in love with Italy hook, line and sinker. I had the melody 'Isle of Capri' on my brain.

Chapter 6
My Dolce Vita

M y first trip to Italy had such an effect on me – the way people interacted with each other with ease and attention, the weather, the endless panoramas and views, the way the architecture was built into the landscape and the language, which I took to easily. In 1955 I decided to live in Italy and this coincided with another bee in my bonnet, which was to become a proper grown-up, someone who could manage to be independent in the adult world. At twenty-three it was high time. I had already secured a job in Rome at the FAO – the Food and Agricultural Organization, a branch of the United Nations. I stayed for almost five years, with regular visits to England in between.

The purpose of the FAO is bold and clear: to eradicate hunger and malnutrition worldwide. To this end, its agricultural, fisheries and forestry programmes are all concerned with the same goal: the sustainability of food production. There are some ideological goals of behaviour and attitudes tucked in as well. It is fair to say FAO is about improving the world and it is highly regarded.

It was miraculous for me, and a privilege and luxury. We

were diplomats and VIPs who needed no visas. The salaries were high and the holidays generous. There were also a lot of perks and it was very easy to live within one's means. Probably too easy. It was hardly a fair test of coping alone. Lovely apartments were easy to find and affordable to rent, and many English girls were around to share them with. Although in fact, the first flat I rented belonged to a new Italian friend I was introduced to. She was as beautiful as the day is long, and also so stylishly dressed – as I realised most Roman girls were and I would have to learn.

She wore a yellow cotton dress made of such quality that the fabric had a sheen to it, and open brown sandals. No jewellery – just that. The flat belonged to her brother, an artist who was away in New York being discovered (which he quite quickly was). She was called Mimi Gnoli and was an artist herself. She had many English connections and we are still friends and in contact. The flat in the Via Arenula with a large rooftop terrace was divine, she was a talented gardener. I bought my first car, a tiny second-hand Fiat called Topolino (little mouse). Life in Rome was shaping up to be thrilling and interesting – even more so when I met my first boyfriend.

At the FAO I was hired as a PA and worked mainly in the personnel department – what would be called human resources now. My boss was Italian, a Signor Carlo Buonacorsi with whom I got on very well, and his family spoilt me. I certainly became very knowing about all the staff working there. It was also possible to change to other departments when vacancies occurred, often temporarily. I had a stint in the agriculture department, and the work concerned the dire irrigation problems for the crops in Africa. When I consider this now, more than half a century on, I wonder how it is possible that in certain parts of

Africa people are still without enough food and money to live on (this is quite apart from war-torn areas). It is about profits from crops not going to the local people. I expect we, in Europe, probably benefit from this.

Sadly I did not find the expat life at the FAO as fulfilling as anticipated, despite all the comfortable conditions and interesting people. There was no tight culture; everyone had completely different experiences and nationalities. I didn't know where half of them came from on the world map. It was like living in the VIP lounge at the airport, neither at home nor abroad, belonging nowhere. I had come for Italy and the Italian people, not the whole wide world.

Young Italian males in the 1950s, with their sex-obsessed behaviour, were decidedly very tiresome, and their pestering meant a girl could never sit down alone anywhere, no matter how hot and weary. However, apart from this self-imposed rigmarole of chatting up, which was treated like a sport, there was always Rome itself to talk about.

We were all beguiled by the beautiful, imposing buildings, which changed colour so dramatically according to the light and time of day. The luminosity of the stone (travertine) even altered feelings too. Around the hour before sunset, I heard someone say, '*Questa é la mia ora triste*' – this is my sad hour. I can't imagine these words from an Englishman. I know it sounds melodramatic, but I do understand what he meant. Especially in my pet areas around Piazza del Parlamento and the Pantheon.

A few months later, I met my first boyfriend, who was called Osvaldo, a 25-year-old designer in high-fashion menswear, working in his prestigious family firm. His brother, sister and mother also worked there. The business had been started by his father, when the workshop used to

be a gathering place for his famous clients and intellectuals, which included Aldous Huxley and the film directors
Fellini, Visconti and Antonioni, among others. Always
ahead of the fashion, Osvaldo was ambitious and apparently
he ended up within the top league with his own collection
in collaboration with Giorgio Armani, Nino Cerruti and
other international names.

We went around mostly with his friends in a group. We
also used to meet in the workshop. He didn't actively 'lead',
but he was somehow the one they followed. They were
a cheerful lot, interested in culture; he especially always
loved looking at architecture wherever we went. It was my
first, but not last, penchant for erudite and cultured men.
He was neurotic, slim and witty and he was my type. This
has remained so – I cannot bear a man who has even a
whiff of being pleased with himself. I felt like Beatrice in
Much Ado About Nothing, 'There's not a wise man among
twenty that will praise himself.'

On our excursions to marvellous places in and outside Rome, I found I had never really *looked* at buildings
before, nor knew basic Bible stories or the inside of
churches. Other than frescoes, I had to discover fonts,
reliefs, altarpieces, cupolas, triptychs and much more.
Was the lack of exposure a fault of my own or the English
schooling system?

At weekends we all usually went to the Roman seaside and sometimes on longer trips to Naples, Positano,
Sorrento, Pompeii and Herculaneum. Sightseeing in a
group nearly all the time seemed strange to me, as in
England couples tended to pair off. But slowly I got used
to the fact that there was a pack mentality here that I had
not encountered before. Of course, I also liked it when we

did travel alone. Once I accompanied him on a business trip to Milan.

I was curious to see the Ligurian coast, having till then only been acquainted with the Amalfi one, which I adored, including Naples itself. So we drove all the way back from Milan to Rome, stopping at various places, with huge beaches like Santa Margherita, and also the bijou Portofino. I didn't get to the marvellous city of Genoa until my reincarnation later with Eric – all in the future, and the same was true for Venice. Osvaldo was a wonderful driver and I was never nervous with him, no matter what speed – and *speed* there was! He also came to London with me and met my family, but his lack of English made for sticky conversation. And my mother was in a fluster and my brothers teased me again. Very unusual and unsophisticated behaviour from my family that day. I don't really know why. Maybe it was a shock that Marlene was now with a man, and no longer the little girl who needed their protection.

It was a perfect time to be in Italy. After the war had ended in 1945, it became part of the West. The Marshall Plan helped rebuild the economy and there was huge optimism. Italians didn't just get back on their feet – they flourished profoundly. Gone were the Fascists, gone was Mussolini and in came free elections, and the traditional political parties were somewhat restored: the Christian Democrats and also a popular Communist Party. Italy became a member of NATO, the UN and, later, the EU, and after all the terrible years of repression and dictatorship, Italians were now free to travel themselves and to welcome the world.

America was their saviour and role model, which launched them into free commerce and enterprise. With the contribution of the Agnelli family and the gigantic car production in the north – of Maseratis, Lancias, Lamborghinis, Alfa Romeos, Ferraris and Fiats – it was called 'Il Boom' aka *il miracolo economico*. For the women, it was a revolution, uprooting entire communities. They no longer wanted to spend their lives on the land, tending animals; they yearned for nice clothes and shoes and to work in offices: they wanted the city. The new freedoms also unleashed a fresh creativity in design, fashion and art. Their furniture and domestic products became international and desired. 'Made in Italy' was about to become all the rage. It still is today.

America's influence permeated all sectors of life, but especially the cinema. So Mariella was not the only one with a passion for Hollywood – Rome too was buzzing with it and soon emerged as a major location for film-making, known as 'Hollywood on the Tiber'. The love relationship went both ways; Hollywood had a passion for Italy, creating films there like *Roman Holiday* with Audrey Hepburn and *Three Coins in the Fountain*. Cinecittà (Rome's film studios) brought much attention to the city and to Italian filmmaking, culminating with Fellini's *La Dolce Vita*. One of the popular songs of 1956 was 'Tu vuò fà l'americano' ('You want to pretend you are an American') sung by Renato Carosone.

Everyone was star-struck and tried to catch a glimpse of Ingrid Bergman, Gina Lollobrigida, Anita Ekberg, Monica Vitti, Marcello Mastroianni and Sofia Loren, to name a few. The film stars were hounded by photographers on Vespas, a new phenomenon they later called the 'paparazzi' (after a surname of one of the riders in *La Dolce Vita*). After about three or more years in Rome, I seemed to have widened my circle of acquaintances. It was just as well; at some point there was another girl in Osvaldo's life. The strange thing is that Osvaldo remained as sweet and loving as always with me. I didn't know what or whom to believe, nor what to think. I was not furious with jealousy. I had never expected or really wanted a future with him, though my soft spot for him was always there. Instead I accepted the attentions of a Franco Reggiani. He was distant and rather snobbish, highly educated and keen for us to go out together. He was handsome. He was actually far too chilly for me – I think it was his adorable address that I liked so much: Vicolo del Divino Amore (Little Street of Divine Love) near Piazza Borghese, and now I had an excuse to use it in answer to his little messages.

Franco's sister Alessandra was getting married and I was invited to the wedding in Tuscany. The wedding reception seemed like a cross between a grand opera and a Pieter Bruegel painting. It was held in the grounds of the family farm and in the house.

The staff in colourful clothes were like a chorus, and participated, serving the food and enjoying themselves, albeit knowing their place. The relatives and friends mingled in their city elegance and Alessandra in the simplest white wedding dress with only a decorated veil and no jewellery; she was the most stylish bride I have ever seen, before and since. I talked with an uncle of Franco and the bride, a gentleman called Luxardo Servadio, who said to me that English girls (there were quite a few at the wedding) were too superficial and knew far too little about Italy. Never was there a truer sentence and I liked him so much for coming out with this. It was music to my ears – *so it wasn't just me.* And somehow, in Italy where everything is possible, a group of us arranged to visit Pisa with him, including the famous cemetery and of course right to the top of the Leaning Tower. Luxardo was an adorable guide and a wise and friendly man. He had a passion for history, although he was an industrial chemist by profession. An optimist and most delightful company; we were so very lucky.

Somewhere, sometime later, in a swimming pool, I met one of his daughters, Gaia, who lives in London. She is a writer who has a big heart and feels responsible for Italy – when an important Italian artist or personality is due to arrive in London she prepares to throw a party for them. She is a serious lover of opera and a very colourful person herself. She lives with her second English husband. For me she is a good friend and a link between my girlish and adult Italy.

Chapter 7
The Congo

After my relationship with Osvaldo, I thought it was time to leave Italy, but I was not quite ready to go home just yet. As it happened, there was a crisis in the Congo and the FAO needed staff to work with the UN in Léopoldville, the country's capital, now called Kinshasa. Well, I volunteered. I went home first to see my family in London, and then flew straight to Leopoldville from there. It is a complicated and bitterly tragic story, which I will shorten and omit intricacies, like the synopsis of an *opera seria*. All the main 'characters' are male politicians: the President of the Congo, Joseph Kasavubu (I love pronouncing that surname); Prime Minister Elect, Patrice Lumumba, who was a radical and communist; Secretary General of the United Nations, Dag Hammarskjöld; leader of the Katanga province, Moïse Tschombe; and, lastly, a colonel named Joseph-Désiré Mobutu. After the Congo's independence from Belgium was declared in June 1960, the predictable colonial void appeared, and rebellions began to take place in many provinces. The Belgians sent in troops to restore order, but this only made matters worse and led to even more mutinies. Together, Kasavubu and Lumumba asked the United Nations to send in peacekeeping troops, which Hammarskjöld agreed to do. The Katanga province had the most at stake, as it was the richest province, with the copper belt (and possibly diamonds). Soon the unrest of secessions within secessions and factions within factions began, and then multiplied all over the entire country.

Surely that is enough. But alas not. The situation became much more complicated and dangerous when Lumumba made the decision to seek assistance from the Russians. This of course alarmed the USA and led to that familiar proxy war situation with the Soviet Union. Finally, the unstoppable Colonel Joseph-Désiré Mobutu continued putting himself in charge wherever he could and succeeded in becoming chief of the army.

These are the very basics of the Congo crisis we ouselves spent our evenings playing pontoon in luxury hotels. Were we all involved in an Evelyn Waugh novel, I wondered? I don't know how the journalists managed to file through all the news and piece together the scattered information for their daily articles. Without going into all the tribal factions, I have simplified the complexities of the conflict.

My job was rather interesting. I spent my year there with the UN mission, working in welfare for the UN troops, supplying them with enough books, records and sports equipment, and arranging different leisure activities, film shows and entertainments. I drew the line at umpiring a football match, although I was asked to do that.

The UN personnel and the international press were put up in two hotels in Léopoldville. Mine was the Stanley and the other one was called the Memling.

Once again I found myself in a group. We played cards

(for real money, as counters were among the many things you could not buy any more), read books and just hung out together. My main friends in the foreign press were Gerry Ratzin from Reuters and, more vaguely, a Frenchman from Agence France-Presse.

I was keen to see more of Africa. Luckily, Gerry had to go to Johannesburg to cover a story and was glad for me to tag along with him. We had a very pleasant trip; I even had friends from Manchester living there, who had interesting opinions and stories to tell about their lives in South Africa. They had watched me grow up in Manchester and were very excited about my visit. I soon grew tired of gambling and wanted to travel. I then met a very interesting Belgian (Flemish) girl called Monique Geschier, who had a job at the Telecom (I think she was dealing with priority calls) and she lived in a large, charming flat that came free with her job. She asked me to move in with her, the arrangement being I paid for our daily Congolese housekeeper, David. Monique had been living in the Congo for several years, escaping a very sad family past, including an acrimonious divorce, which ended without access to her two little daughters, who lived in Belgium. We got on famously. She was pretty, with real Titian-coloured hair, and all the men looked at her before me, except for Kamal. I don't remember how I met him; he was a very charming (rather short for me) man from the Ismaili clan, who were followers of the Aga Khan. He must have been the sweetest person I've ever known, and he adored me. Not in the usual way, but as though I was a princess. He didn't dream of going to bed with me. In his culture, that happened with quite different women. But together we were very happy to hold hands and cuddle, and we spent many good evenings with

Monique and her friends. People were very surprised that we saw so much of each other, and so was I. I didn't learn as much as I should have about Ismaili culture and customs. I wish I had done. Kamal knew I wanted to travel, and he recommended I go to East Africa, to Mombasa in Kenya and Tanzania, where he had relatives. One of his cousins actually lived in an apartment in the Sultan's palace in Zanzibar, and I was invited to visit her. Kamal had already written; we had our tea together, followed by the grand tour of the palace – lots of ornate patterns in refined light colours and gold remains in my memory. These patterns were used to decorate everything, from the carpet to the wall, *objets d'art* and more. I can see why Matisse wanted to travel there. I spent all my time sightseeing the island, people watching and necklace shopping. The world, as far as I was concerned, felt safe, though I knew it was also terrible. No thoughts, of course, about terrorism. It was just a different era, and a time when I felt completely free and extremely content, perhaps, dare I say, even grown-up. This was just as well, as it turned out to be the last big time on my own. I couldn't peep into the future. Back in the Congo I was soon reminded we were in a war zone. Mobutu, again with his machinations, had pulled off yet another coup and as head of the army (and with the new compliance of Kasavubu) put Lumumba under house arrest. Guarded by Ghanian UN troops, Lumumba escaped but was recaptured and sent to Katanga, where he was tortured and executed under the authority of Tshombe. It was barbaric, as there was absolutely no legal process whatsoever for all this. The deed was just carried out. There were certainly strong worldwide protests and demonstrations, but all to no avail. We were in the middle of the Cold

War and no one would speak up for a communist. Even at the United Nations there were not enough votes to take it up. Dag Hammarskjöld was killed in a plane crash, along with his bodyguard, who was also my friend. There were rumours of foul play. With his new alliances, Mobutu became a dictator and stayed in power for years, changing the name of the country to Zaire in 1971. Monique was well connected with the Congolese elite, diplomats and interesting Belgians. I remember she took me to a grand garden party where Mobutu slowly walked towards me and asked me personally if I would be willing to give him English lessons, which I had the common sense and savoir faire to carefully decline.

My year was up and I was ready to go home. Monique came with me and she stayed with us until she found a suitable job. She was very keen on archaeology and it was not long before she found an excellent one working with the team under Kathleen Kenyon – at the time very famous for her excavations in Jericho – on a new expedition. It was the jackpot for her. Later on, she married the director of the Archaeological Institute of America in Chicago, where she still lives. She was reunited with her girls and had a son.

Chapter 8
Back Home and CBC

I came home to London in 1961 and worked for the Canadian Broadcasting Corporation (CBC) in the newsroom as PA to the news supervisor of Europe, Garran Patterson. I got this exciting, well-paid job in central London through my good friend Hannah Horrowitz, who did freelance work at CBC. Hannah was a musical agent and impresario, and very well connected. Our office was in the Langham Buildings, once a hotel, but at the time part of the BBC and situated across the road from Broadcasting House. It is now a hotel again. Our noisy, lively newsroom was always full of journalists staying or passing through; I remember Morley Safer and Roméo LeBlanc particularly. Every day their wisecracks and opinions made me feel we were taking part in an excellent play. I loved my job, starting daily with a telephone conversation to Diana Fowler, a Canadian in the Paris office, about the schedules for the day.

Much later, when I left CBC to prepare for my first child, Diana took over my job and we became friends for life. She married the boss and, as Mrs Patterson, brought two little girls into the world. But after two decades, the marriage ended and she returned to live in Canada. There she eventually married Roméo LeBlanc, who became the governor general, making her the viceregal consort; in other words the First Lady of Canada. No kidding! I still have the video of his installation. There she was – *my* Diana – on the world stage and doing a very good job of it too.

Chapter 9
Meeting Eric

When I met Eric Hobsbawm he was a groovy single man about town, much in demand socially, as he was known to be good company. He was an offbeat academic and very friendly with his students, teaching history in the evenings at Birkbeck College. As well as writing history books, he was a journalist on all manner of subjects, writing reviews and articles, including a jazz column in the *New Statesman*. For this, he had to hang out in clubs in Soho, including strip bars, and he acquired a pseudonym, Francis Newton, to make sure his students only asked him questions about history. He had been a member of the Communist Party since his schoolboy days in Berlin in 1931.

My brother Walter now had a wife, Dorothy Morgan. They were already raising a family, living in Hampstead Garden Suburb, and I spent a fair amount of my spare time with them. Dorothy was a mature student at Birkbeck College and Eric was her supervisor. Walter and Dorothy gave a dinner party, and 'Walter's sister' and 'Dorothy's supervisor' were both invited. That's how Eric and I met. I think the chemistry between us was there right from the beginning. Neither of us could recollect any of the other guests present, though they were definitely there. Eric had a beautiful tenor speaking voice I was attracted to, and his eyes hardly left me, even when he was engaged in conversation with other guests.

Something definitely changed in me after that evening in November 1961. I remember being bothered that Eric had said he was going off on a trip soon. I was living temporarily in my brother Victor's flat in Mansfield Street, London W1. He'd gone away on a journey and had lent me his gorgeous place until he returned. I shared it with two girlfriends and we decided to organise a dinner party (my idea), each of us inviting a male friend.

While I have a vague recollection of that evening, it is a different memory that still stays with me: I was the first of us to telephone the other, and Eric was very enthusiastic about accepting the invitation. Yes indeed, he was free to come to the dinner in a week's time, but wanted to know what I was doing *now* this very minute. I dodged that word *now*. This was the early sixties, when nice girls would feel it was too fast to doing something like go along with him to help buy groceries for his flat as a first date. Had it been in the 1970s, after seeing those engaging Woody Allen films, I might have easily have accepted.

The fact is, he was supposed to be in Cuba with a group of intellectuals at a conference also attended by Fidel Castro and Che Guevara. He was looking forward to talking with the other travellers, particularly the activist and writer Arnold Kettle and the theatre director Joan Littlewood. But there was a fault on the plane discovered at Prague and they had to return to London. Eric felt very fed up about his wasted time, about his empty diary and at having no provisions at home. At the exact moment when he gloomily stepped into his flat, I telephoned. It was a lucky start. The stars were aligned. Eric's aborted trip to Cuba did take place in the new year.

When Vic returned from his travels, I moved back into my Paddington Street attic flat over a fishmonger's (now a boutique), and Eric and I began to see each other quite often. What did we do? Like millions of others, we talked about ourselves, and being forty-five and twenty-nine, there was plenty to say. Eric had even been married! Goodness me. His classes were three evenings a week and the other evenings we often tried to meet, going out to supper, cinema, concerts and so on, until simply, 'Your place or mine?'

Eric introduced me to an architect, Martin Frishman and his mother Margaret, a painter. We became firm friends and his mother painted a picture of my father and later another one of Eric. Both were traditional and beautiful large oil portraits. Unlike *La Bohème*, this was my introduction to *haute bohème*. Martin's large studio flat was in Belgravia, and the previous tenant had been Noel Coward. Martin told me that the difference between bohemians and other people was that bohemians wash their dishes before they eat rather than after. Many of Eric's friends were artists like these.

I wanted to introduce Eric to my cousin Peter Nettl, with whom I had always got on very well and who sometimes invited me on family holidays and business trips. I remember good times in Sardinia and Cairo with them. Peter had left academia to become a businessman, and had written a very fine biography of Rosa Luxemburg, the activist murdered by anti-communist paramilitaries

in Germany in 1919. He was thrilled that I was going out
with Eric. I gave a small dinner party in my flat at which
Peter commented on Eric's telling way of carving a roast
leg of lamb. He insisted that despite his fluent German, Eric
would be a useless spy, as all would know he could not be
anything but an Englishman. Eric, Peter and I could not
remain friends for life because, to our perpetual horror,
Peter was killed in a Northwest Airlines' plane crash some
years later in America. His wife Marietta and three others
survived the crash. Their daughter Andrea, now a true
culture vulture and a Wagnerian, is and has been my friend
since she was seven years old.

Eric was often away, either abroad or at universities
around the country, mainly giving papers for seminars.
Absences seemed to make the heart grow fonder and our
merry dating life continued for almost a year. However,
there was a glitch. Eric had won a very generous grant from
the Rockefeller Foundation to travel around Latin America
for three months to continue his research into 'primitive
rebels', a concept that he had used as the title for his second
book, but was still investigating. Suddenly this sharpened
our minds; to avoid the shock of such a very long separation, things ought to move swiftly between us.

Our relationship was known to Walter and Dorothy,
but not as yet to my parents. The person I confided in was
Gretl Lenz, who was a very special cousin and also my
mother's best friend. Gretl had always played a crucial role
in all our lives since we were little in the old Vienna days,
and she was very often amongst us, always living nearby;
we all loved her and never wanted her to go home to her
difficult husband and dachshunds, but she did. I suppose
Gretl's name must have been chosen because her brother's

middle name was Hans – maybe a touch of Austrian humour. She did not have children, but was very family minded and close to her high-flying international lawyer brother and his very English wife Barbara and, above all, their beloved daughter Patsy, who has always been a close cousin. Gretl's wisdom was always spot on and quick. I took Eric to meet her first. They got on famously and she paved the way for us.

One evening I accompanied Eric to the George Shearing jazz quintet at the Royal Festival Hall, which he was covering for the *New Statesman*. He said something very unromantic like, 'I think we should take out our diaries and find time for a wedding before I have to leave.' That was the proposal and there was certainly no bent knee. It was, however, not so simple, because a register office had to be booked at least three weeks in advance for a wedding. That was a shame, and the only way we could arrange it was to go on our two-week honeymoon *first*, have our wedding *second*, and Eric would leave for his research trip *third*. For the honeymoon we had decided on Bulgaria, straight to Sofia via Vienna, which included a night at the opera, and then on to the small, charming resort Golden Sands on the Black Sea. Eric was delighted to see some people there reading Pushkin out loud to one another in the square.

More or less as soon as we got back in October 1962, we married at Marylebone register office. Martin Frishman was our best man and a reception followed at my parents' house. The next day we went on a short second honeymoon. Vic had gracefully lent us his car for the weekend and we drove to Castle Combe in Wiltshire. Eric told me how scared he was of marriage.

He snobbishly connected it with having boring holidays in a caravan by the seaside.

Five days after our return to London, Eric was off. Before embarking, a man at the airport asked, 'Is your father also going to Buenos Aires?' It made me laugh. I had not yet started on Eric's wardrobe and that unflattering greenish coloured coat (ugh!) made him look as old as Methuselah.

Leaping ahead nearly half a century, I can tell you another man who must have been there at the airport. He was from MI5, where it was discovered that Eric's research trip was sponsored by the American Rockefeller Foundation. They sent this man to spy on Eric, presumably for his US contacts. All of this was revealed in a fascinating article by Frances Stonor Saunders in the *London Review of Books*[3] when Eric's MI5 file became viewable in 2015. Eric had so much wanted to see his MI5 file, but permission was always refused. Martin Jacques, editor of *Marxism Today* and also an intimate family friend, accompanied me to view the files when they were released. It certainly made dispiriting reading. It seems the spooks disliked Eric intensely. They didn't approve of his looks or his clothes, and there were a few anti-Semitic remarks. More than that, I think they hated him because they had not been able to find anything on him. And that, quite simply, was because there was nothing to find. What did they expect? Surely an open member of the Communist Party, who wore this proudly on his sleeve, would hardly be a spy. But they went on digging.

All throughout our two honeymoons and one wedding,

3   April 2015, vol. 37, no. 7.

we were in the middle of the Cuban Missile Crisis, with the US and Russia on the brink of war. It was just beginning to settle, but Eric's last words to me before he flew off were, 'Should things go wrong and war does break out, then buy a one-way ticket to Argentina. There is enough money in the bank and I'll meet you in Buenos Aires.'

OH! Heart pumping, I had not reckoned with that. Did I *really* know my man well enough? But life had fallen into my lap, and I was just going to live it. I think that was how I felt.

Chapter 10
Being Married

I began my married life as a wife alone, my new husband being somewhere in Latin America, but I was not sure where. I had already moved into Eric's flat in Bloomsbury, Gordon Mansions in Huntley Street, and I continued working in the CBC newsroom. We wrote to each other most days. Letters were crucial as the telephone was too expensive, and in any case our phone was tapped and hardly suitable for the talk of separated lovers. The phone tapping started when Guy Burgess (part of the infamous spy circle, the Cambridge Five) phoned Eric from Moscow as a lark to say he couldn't come to the Cambridge Apostles Dinner and would Eric please make his excuses. After that, there was always the telling click on our phone. A couple of months after Eric left, I threw a party for a few colleagues and friends, which turned out to be quite noisy. Suddenly the phone rang and it was Eric's cousin Denis Preston. Hearing all the voices, he said, 'Are you throwing a party? Sounds very noisy. Ought you to be partying with your husband away?' Oh dear, I thought I had put my foot in it with Eric's family, but he was only teasing. Little did I know then that

Denis, who had introduced Eric to jazz in the first place, was the unstuffiest and most swinging relative he had. It was however, a very crucial and timely wake-up call for me. I needed to inspect the flat more sensibly and to sort things out, especially in the kitchen, as it was a stark reminder that fairly soon proper meals would have to be cooked in there every day – by me! Blimey!

For three months I had waited patiently for Eric's return like Cio-Cio San (in *Madame Butterfly*) and now it was time to distribute the cherry blossoms. His return was such a relief. We were bursting with joy. And I was pregnant with our honeymoon baby.

Eric and I had already met many of each other's relatives. My parents liked Eric, my mother especially. I knew Eric's sister Nancy, her husband Victor and their three children, Robin, Anne and Jeremy, as well as Eric's close cousin Ronnie, his wife Mary and their daughter Angela. None of them lived in London, so we saw much less of them than my relatives, although when Angela and her family moved to London, they also visited, like all the relations. My brother Vic, always concerned about his little sister, had already made enquiries through his old boys' network about Eric's Communist Party membership, but he was assured that the spooks already knew all about him as an open and declared communist.

Of course, I knew that Eric had been married before, to Muriel Seaman. I also knew that when the marriage dissolved, Eric had had an affair with Marion Bennathan, a mature psychology student, and was the father of her child, Joss. Marion insisted she wanted to keep this a secret, because it would not be fair to her husband, Ezra, and Eric obeyed. Nonetheless Eric would visit Joss from time to time, usually at Christmas to take him to a show, like an uncle.

Eric started to introduce me to his cosmopolitan and English friends and I did the same. I met all manner of remarkable people through Eric. It was one of the best things in my life with him. Our friends were hugely important for both of us. They played a crucial role throughout our married life. They were so close to us and such an important part of our lives even when not present.

When we started meeting each other's friends, Eric was keen that we go to Cambridge first because his friends were very curious about me, having convinced themselves Eric would never marry again. Gabriele Annan and her husband Noel, provost of King's College, had invited us for lunch at the Provost's Lodge. I'm fairly certain the art historian Francis Haskell, a bosom friend of Eric's and of the Annans, was also there. I cannot recollect the others. Later Gaby told me she expected Eric to arrive with a sort of a red battleaxe. The Annans were very chic, both dressed in casual but elegant clothes, with Noel in a bright pink shirt. They welcomed me with huge warmth and friendliness, which immediately lifted my diffidence at university gatherings. Usually when asked what field I was in, I would have to resist the temptation to say, 'The one with the bull in it.' I had no field, nor subject. As yet. A decade later I was able to hold my own as a music teacher. A great relief all round for conversation at formal university dinners when my new label, *Music Teacher*, solved everything, starting with the card at my place setting.

The sophisticated Annans, of course, could converse on all topics, but many dons were at a complete loss when not talking about college affairs, which really surprised me. We became close to Gaby and Noel; they often invited us and we them. Gaby was very keen on company, partly because she feared boredom; so much so I think it was a phobia. She told me it sprang from her suffering as a lonely child having to endure long adult dinners. Much of our talk was usually about Cambridge friendships or the arts. Noel joked about how he and Eric were both members of political groups, one advocating communism, the other gay rights. In his plummy voice, he said, 'My dear Eric, you were in the Comintern; I was in the Homintern.' Gaby and Noel were a close family with two friendly, high–flying daughters Lucy and Juliet.

We discovered marriage was good for us; at last there was a routine and a rhythm to our lives, which neither of us had had for years. The institution of marriage itself suited us even though it was slightly going out of fashion amongst our artistic crowd. Our friend and poet Erich Fried said to his partner (the sculptor Catherine Boswell), 'Don't worry – I promise to marry you before I divorce you.'

I was head over heels in love with Eric; he was everything to me, and on top of all of that I was in awe of him. Quite a load. Once I apparently put my finger to my lips and whispered to an Italian guest at supper, 'Shh, he is speaking.' I only learned about this gaffe years later, and we both roared with laughter. Eric was in love too, but I think I was perhaps too bourgeois for him to actually let himself go crazy for me. He had never had a steady relationship before, let alone a woman who would produce initialled linen from her mother's trousseau. But his big love did come; it grew little by little until one day, a few years down the line, he said he didn't really enjoy going to places any more without me by his side. I often wondered what it was that bound us together for ever. We were now sophisticated, grown-up cosmopolitans, but in our own sealed selves I think at times we both felt like displaced people, although we never really talked seriously about this to each other. Those who know about Eric's childhood from his autobiography *Interesting Times* would, I think, understand.

Life in Bloomsbury was very easy for us – being able to walk to most places in the West End, including the Jazz club Ronnie Scott's at night. Not to mention the convenience of living on the same street as the University College Hospital maternity unit. It was a charmed life indeed, but it didn't last that long. Eric was incredibly busy with academia and writing. I discovered I was to share him with the world. Already historians came from many countries to talk to him. He liked it this way, to learn from people he trusted about what was happening in their part of the world. He was a good listener and listened hard. These visitors went mostly to Birkbeck, but old friends and those who knew him well came to the flat, and I got roped in. We soon needed to buy some new crockery. After all, we were living in a single man's flat.

Then Eric's book *The Age of Revolution* (the first in the *Ages* series), published by Weidenfeld & Nicolson, came out. It was mostly very well received, both in England and internationally. All at once, publishers had propositions for Eric and professors from all over the place wanted him to come and lecture. Eric's reputation had suddenly shifted. He did not even have a literary agent yet. That's when it all started to be a bit chaotic for him and I gave in my notice at CBC.

Chapter 11
A New Family

O f course we had talked about having children. Actually, Eric adored babies and toddlers. He could not resist making funny faces and noises for them whenever we were travelling on trains or planes. Sometimes it was embarrassing or they wailed when he stopped, which he hadn't predicted. But that was a world apart from the responsibility of raising children.

I discovered that Eric didn't (or, rather, couldn't) lie. It was a revelation. Nothing to do with morality: he was simply not cunning enough. All of us have different levels of feelings and emotions; Eric's seemed fathomless and he wanted to be in touch with what he felt – almost like a dialogue to get at the truth. I think this interfered with being able to simulate or tell a lie easily (naturally, this is only my theory). He told me he would have preferred to have me all to himself, easily able to travel the world together. He also knew, which I did not, how much support serious writers needed. However, having said all this to me, he was also very much Eric the pragmatist *par excellence*. He knew, and had already said, that it was not possible to marry a young and healthy woman, and expect her to compromise hopes of motherhood. He said he was in for the 'whole package'. And in any case, once our children arrived; he was smitten.

In June 1963 our son Andy (Andrew John) decided it was time to enter the world. We were having lunch with cousin Denis in nearby Charlotte Street when I went into labour, and Denis immediately drove us to University College Hospital, pulling my leg as usual – 'Marlene, you are not to mess up my new car' – a joke that had the three of us giggling inappropriately when we arrived at the reception for the maternity unit. Andy was born in the evening, and I became the proud mother of the longest baby measured on the ward. Eric said, 'Oh my God, he looks just like Uncle Sidney.' Mothers normally stayed in hospital for ten days at that time, mainly to learn how to bathe their babies properly, and we all had to be supervised doing this. The NHS was responsible for everything, including daily physiotherapy. They sent us home with equipment and feeling pretty confident. And even then, they came to our homes to see if all was going smoothly.

It turned out Bloomsbury was a lovely place with a baby, especially in June. We were so near the shops and could walk with the pram to Charlotte Street and sit outside at restaurants with our friends as if on the Continent. There was the pretty Gordon Square garden, to which we had a key and where all sorts of interesting mums were also minding their children. I remember the enjoyment of chatting with the writer Antonia Byatt, for one. The only big snag was the many outside steps up to our mansion flat. Every day I was haunted by the image of the pram rolling down the steps like in *Battleship Potemkin*. Later, when

Andy was old enough to sit upright, Eric liked to walk around Russell Square with him in a new baby contraption strapped on his shoulders, showing him the world: not surprisingly Andy's first word was, 'Look-at-that,' with his finger pointing. Andy was a healthy and strong baby who soon grew into a very handsome one. He was easy about everything other than accepting new solid food.

We took him to France when he was barely a toddler to stay with Anne and John Willett (man of multiple letters) at their place Le Thiel near Dieppe. To me it seemed that Andy refused to eat anything for the entire week. I went into the garden, clueless as to whether those green tops were carrots or turnips, parsnips or whatever else. I cleaned, cooked and puréed them, but he immediately spat everything out. He was on a hunger strike, I think. In spite of enjoying ourselves so much with the Willetts, whose company we always coveted, Andy's fasting made us mighty glad when our week's stay was up. It was a shame. Our second child was planned. It was Eric who insisted it would be unfair for Andy not to have a sibling. Especially on our travels, the children would need each other. And he was right. It turned out there was only fourteen months age difference between them and they were very close, and have stayed so. This has always been the root of my happiness. Today they both live with their own families, raising their children in houses within a mile from one another. That is, of course, quite normal in families all over the world, but in Jewish families in the twenty-first century I consider it a small miracle. We hoped for a girl and I had only chosen girls' names. In the daytime of 15 August 1964, again across the road in Huntley Street, our daughter Julia Nathalie arrived. She was not at all like Uncle Sidney, and a little rosy. She was named Julia because I so loved the street La Via Giulia in Rome, and Nathalie was a charming French girl, daughter of my parents' Parisian friends, the Jouard family, whom we admired during my teenage years. My day now started with the 5.20 a.m. shipping forecast, pondering over Dogger, Cromarty, Fair Isle, Fastnet Lundy, Finisterre, German Bight and Bailey. I was also reading Doris Lessing's *The Grass is Singing,* a marvellous account of her life in southern Rhodesia (now Zimbabwe) and I would recommend it wholeheartedly, even without simultaneously feeding a baby in a silent, unheated flat. Life with two children under two years needed some ingenuity. My bright idea was to hire an au pair, a pleasant Dutch girl. She liked to walk as far as Trafalgar Square with Andy in a pushchair because he had become so excited looking at the pigeons and eventually running with them. He insisted on going there every day. He was too little to be very upset or jealous by Julia's arrival, although one day I did see a large toy brick placed in his sister's cot exactly where her head would have been! I spent my afternoons pushing Julia in the pram. With Andy I was told babies should lie on their tummies, which I obeyed, but I didn't with Julia. I preferred her to be on her back so I could see her and she was able to see me too. Much more fun. In all these events, grandmothers who are able to often play a role, and my mother (now Grandma Lilly) was no exception. She would leave wonderfully cooked Gefüllte Paprika (stuffed peppers) or goulash dishes outside our flat door so as not to disturb us. She already had her hands full with my father's Parkinson's disease and his old age, but she made time for us too. At weekends I always had somewhere to go – my parents' warm and welcoming home in Golders Green. The children would play in the garden there and sometimes their little cousins came.

Chapter 12

Clapham, Part I
Cottage in Wales and Massachusetts

T he pram, the pushchair, the high chair, the playpen: the stuff was crushing us and we began to contemplate buying a house. We had a stroke of luck. Our friends, Alan Sillitoe the novelist and his wife, the poet Ruth Fainlight, wanted to buy a large, handsome Victorian house in Clapham and they were looking for a family to share it with. They found the Hobsbawms. It was in the Old Town of Clapham, the least gentrified area, only just beginning to come up, and the house was cheap enough to enable some fine refurbishments by our architect Max Neufeld, who divided the house into two L-shaped maisonettes. It worked out well because of the generous proportions of the house, with its large windows. Our children were barely three and four when we moved in and David Sillitoe was five. It did not turn out to be a lifetime house, neither for the Sillitoes nor for us. I remember a passer-by asked me when the playschool would open – looking through the window and seeing all the books and toys, it didn't cross her mind that the space could be just for one family. The large garden was a dream for the children, and we shared Doreen the cleaner with the Sillitoes. She was a saint, and did babysitting too.

People also wondered what Alan did for money, because he didn't go out to work. They assumed he had won the Pools. It never occurred to them that he could be a writer successful enough to earn a living. He wrote profusely and brought out a book every year, which were all translated into many languages. Later, two of his books, *Saturday Night and Sunday Morning* and *The Loneliness of the Long Distance Runner*, were on the O-level and A-level syllabus for years, and made into successful films, which must have been good news for the family.

During our time in Clapham three tragedies followed one after the other. First, Alan's sister, a mother of four, was diagnosed with cancer. Her youngest child, six-year-old Susan, stayed with Ruth and Alan for a short visit while her mother was receiving treatment. I remember her when she knocked on our garden door once or twice hoping to play with Andy and Julia. She was a lovely and lively little girl. At some stage, after her mother died in 1968, she was adopted by Alan and Ruth.

The Sillitoes decided to go abroad for a year to Mallorca, where they often spent time staying near their great friend, the poet Robert Graves. They rented their Clapham home to an interesting American couple, George and Natalie, who had adopted one little girl called Hannah and were awaiting their second adopted baby. Unfortunately she arrived from America at exactly the same time as Natalie's mother, who expected the full tourist VIP treatment of visits to the theatre, sightseeing and out-of-town places.

Neither the mother nor the new baby could now be postponed.

I secretly thought the new baby was sometimes out in her pram in the garden far too long, but I didn't want to interfere. I also knew that too many different people were looking after her while Natalie and her mother went out: Doreen, George and myself were all tiptoeing around this situation. About two weeks later, the little baby girl died in the night. Andy and Julia woke us up with excitement that an ambulance and a police car were outside. George asked me to take the children, including Hannah, out for the day, as the formal proceedings were going to take a long time. With sandwiches, drinks, a frisbee and a ball, I drove them to Battersea Park.

It was a long day sitting on a bench and my nerves were in shreds, my thoughts unable to stop dwelling on the fact that the baby had shown signs of being ill, which had not been followed up. The blame I felt at my silence and non-intervention was a great source of anxiety for me. I thought I was developing a bad cold, but the next day it turned out to be shingles or Bell's palsy. I could not shut my left eye at all and the left corner of my mouth was also paralysed. During this time Eric had been preparing two lectures to deliver in America the following week. But as Mr Pragmatist, he simply phoned the university without a nanosecond's thought and told them his wife was ill and he couldn't come. This was done and settled, but of course the baby's death lingered. I felt so sorry for them all. The police did not delve much and on the certificate 'cot death' was written. Alan and Ruth allowed George and Natalie to stay longer because of their tragedy. The Sillitoes never returned there, and eventually bought a house in Kent.

My palsy lasted a few months, but alas not my regrets, which are still with me. I went around looking like Long John Silver with a black eyepatch. Eric was in the mood to whisk me off to the most famous hospitals in the world – names like the Mayo Clinic, Leningrad and even Japan were glamorously bandied about, but it turned out the Mecca for neurological diseases was in London's own Queen's Square, and one had but to take the 59 bus to get there. It was both a let-down and a relief.

The last tragedy was the death of our good friend Charlotte Jenkins, who was much too young to die, leaving behind her husband Peter (a *Guardian* correspondent) and her ravishing four-year-old daughter Amy. I had not been to a funeral of someone my age before. I was affected by the beauty of the mourners, many of them young parents, as well as the tributes, especially Jane Miller reading George Herbert's poem 'Life'. Amy was Julia's favourite playmate, and on one occasion when I was collecting her, she turned back and said, 'Goodbye, my beautiful glass mummy.' Amy had recognised her frailty. Children have a way of knowing, even if they don't understand.

Sometimes Eric got exhausted from overwork, and the best thing was to spend a few days away. One of these trips was to North Wales to visit his friend from Cambridge, a Kingsman called Robin Gandy. He was a kind, eccentric and jolly mathematician who spent his holidays in a tiny cottage called Pendomen in the Croesor Valley. It was not far from the foothills of Snowdon on the estate of Clough Williams-Ellis and his wife Amabel, who liked to rent out their houses and cottages to intellectuals and people they knew. Robin had been a friend of Clough and Amabel's son Kitto at Cambridge, and after Kitto was killed in the war, Robin had remained close to his friend's parents.

The famous Italianate village of Portmeirion, which Clough had created, was nearby, and tenants on the estate had the advantage of using it freely and going to the seaside, which had private beaches and a pool, while also living in the wild countryside. Maybe because he now had children, Eric thought how good it would be to have a cottage there too. He asked Robin to recommend him to Clough (a necessity in order to rent) and we hoped something would turn up. Robin must have hit the right tone, giving Eric a glowing review. He soon phoned to tell us a rental cottage had been found and we had first refusal. It was extremely exciting – with short notice at the end of July we managed to farm out the children and the au pair for three days to stay with my mother while we drove up to Merioneth (now Gwynedd) to view the cottage Bryn Hyfryd in the Croesor valley. It was the last cottage in a little row of four. Modest, ordinary and not particularly charming, but you could go out of the back door and the children would be able to run, nearly fly, as far as the eye could see on safe green fields and with magnificent views. There was a little stream nearby. Three bedrooms and bathroom upstairs, with kitchen and living room downstairs.

We were so fixated on arranging to rent the cottage that we almost forgot about picking up the children from Grandma Lilly as promised. We drove fast, suddenly noticing there was no traffic at all. We didn't have a radio. Had something awful happened? A war broken out? Was there a nuclear alert? So engrossed were we in our private affairs, we had forgotten the World Cup at Wembley, where for the first time ever we actually beat the Germans. The TV audience was over 32 million viewers, making it the largest ever (in the UK). It was 30 July 1966. It was to be our first house in Wales and we would have ten years of holidays in it. In the summers, we frequented auctions to buy furniture – Welshmen with their gift of the gab were brilliant auctioneers and knew their role as witty entertainers also made for higher bids. The walks from the house were stunning. Our children learned to climb and loved it. Eric had a ploy – he would tell them they could rest whenever they wanted to, having discovered that they could not sit still for more than a few minutes. There were all sorts of day excursions by car as well (apart from those to Portmeirion), with one memorable visit to Harlech Castle in particular. I don't recommend taking a few children there, as they will inevitably run in different directions shouting, 'Look at me! Look at me!' from the edge of the parapets. I thought I was going to have a heart attack. I enjoyed a long whisky later that night to celebrate coming home with the same number of children that I set off with.

Julia has retained her love of walking and climbing from those days. Andy went in for the more modern running or speed walking.

Then came a surprise. Eric was invited to take a six-month visiting professorship at the prestigious Massachusetts Institute of Technology (MIT) in Boston, USA. We were both very keen to go, especially as this was the time to travel, when the children were not yet in school. Visas for communists were not possible, and a waiver was required. This took time. We carried on with our lives.

I bought a second-hand upright piano in order to refresh my childhood Grade 1-, 2- and 3-level pieces, and to play simple nursery songs and games for the children and their friends (our family baby grand piano had gone to Walter and he deserved it). We were slowly preparing for the trip and the ad we put in the *Guardian* for an au pair brought us over *sixty* replies! Eric simplified the decision, saying we should choose an Irish girl, as the Boston area is full of Irish families; indeed, Phil (the girl we chose) did have relatives there and we felt much relieved. It was a success. When I later asked Phil what made her decide to come with us, she said, 'I took one look at Andy's soft brown doe eyes and decided I just had to take care of him.'

MIT wanted students and teachers from all the sciences, including astrophysics, to attend a history course. They were encouraged to improve and expand their minds through interdisciplinary studies. The name of Eric's course, as I recall, was 'Comparative History'. Eric was certainly going to deliver that.

The waiver issue eventually loomed very large in our lives; MIT eased our worries by assuring us that if the worst came to the worst, they would still pay his full salary for the six months. For a day we toyed with the idea that this might not be so bad – 'Where in Europe shall we go?' I think a power battle between MIT and the FBI immigration had begun. MIT were certainly ready to show the bureaucrats that communist backgrounds did not flummox them and they knew precisely which scholars they wanted to be invited.

Eric had already decided ages before that although he very much wanted to visit American universities, for their heterodoxy especially, he would never vow he had not been a communist in order to do so. He would just not go. So when the waiver arrived he was very pleased that MIT had stuck their neck out for him. He could keep his resolution and travel. Academic vanity also raised its head, I suppose. He wanted to prove that he could continue his work successfully while remaining a communist, even during the Cold War. I think these were his internal monologues and remained so.

Around February of 1967, off we went to the real America; quite different from Manhattan, with its hub of all nationalities and lots of characters looking like Albert Einstein. There had been some difficulty in finding us a house, and we ended up in the suburb of Arlington, about thirty minutes by bus from downtown Boston. People there were a mixture of middle- and working-class Americans. Thinking back fifty years, perhaps some of them might have become Donald Trump voters.

Andy went to a playschool for four-year-olds in the mornings, although he spent most of his time on the bus, being the first child to be picked up and the last to be dropped off. But he was happy and loved chatting with all his new bus friends. Julia stayed at home with Phil and me, both of us often in stitches at her determination to do what she had planned to do, aged three. I had time to practise the recorder and there was also a piano.

I enjoyed our modest life in Arlington. It was temporary and no big decisions had to be taken. Eric was very content because academia at MIT was new and different and therefore a novelty – nothing pleased him more than that. And there were many very agreeable colleagues at MIT and also new faces, like Noam Chomsky. I never got my head around his theory of linguistics, but his political views were wonderful and brave. He was a lovely person and said he would visit us in London.

*

We needed to go to California – Eric was pining to see his great friend Ralph Gleason, who lived in Berkeley with his wife Jeannie. Ralph was a thin, wiry New York Irishman whom Eric had admired and befriended in his New York jazz days in the late fifties. He was now a journalist for the *San Francisco Chronicle*, covering all showbiz and pop music – not a typical friendship match for a middle-aged historian, but you will have gathered that Eric was not typical. When we went to visit, Ralph was reviewing a huge concert, which we were also going along to. At the time, it was the famous 'Summer of Love', which one could write reams about, but I won't. In a nutshell, it was a revolution: an emancipation of the young, who wanted to be done with the forties and fifties, and express themselves differently. They came from across America and beyond to San Francisco, and the epicentre of it all was in the suburb of Haight-Ashbury. The 'hippy trail', as it was called, was also through Europe and the Middle East to India. The hippies dressed in flowery fashion, wanted free love and sex, and took hallucinatory drugs, mainly LSD. Dropping out of conventional society was a new experience, as was their enthusiasm for communal living and a vegetarian diet. This was part of the counterculture that they yearned and strived for.

The music, came out of jazz, but with a different kind of sound, with the most famous performers being the Beatles, the Rolling Stones, Bob Dylan, Jimi Hendrix, Pink Floyd, Ravi Shankar and others. We had come for a very big concert in a huge ballroom called the Fillmore Auditorium, near the Golden Gate Park. It took place just before the gigantic and more famous Monterey Pop Festival. Sitting with the other journalists, Ralph and Eric were further behind me, Jeannie and their teenage children. Aside from the pink psychedelic strobe lighting swirling around (which I did like), the enormous crowds and unbearably loud, slushy music made me nervous.

None of us were on drugs, not even the Gleason teenagers. And so I expect we experienced it very differently from the crowds. I felt a million miles away from Eric, not knowing how he was reacting to all this. When we had a conversation later, I found out that Eric had also not enjoyed it except for the Motown Girls. In his usual way, he had been trying to analyse the evolution of this genre, from jazz, then rock to 'flower-power' music. He said it was probably not possible to get into it without drugs and he also disliked the overamplification. Above all, he felt silly: 'This is for the young. I shouldn't be here.' What a relief. I felt the same.

It was easy to restore my spirits privately. All I had to do was to think of Arlington, where in a couple of days I would see my babes again. We had of course spoken to them, and said we would be bringing presents. But longing always seems more intense towards the very end.

On our return, we decided to do more sightseeing with the children. We had already visited the Boston Aquarium, which was a big hit with Andy. Julia liked it and said some of the teeth were big – Eric was the most enthusiastic of all. I was more fond of the stylish provincial towns in Massachusetts, like Concorde, Lincoln and Lexington; the plain churches were especially impressive. The children were good sightseers, running up and down heaps of museum steps – 'Look here!' and 'Look there!' – and then off to the souvenir shops. They already knew all the culture routines at three and four!

I thought American academics were wonderful people, the best of the best, maybe because they didn't have the same class baggage as in England, and they were modest. But figuring out the Americans I met every day was more difficult. Sometimes there seemed to be a hidden inferiority complex, almost a need to justify themselves, and they expected our impressions of their country to be totally 100 per cent positive. Maybe their sensitivity was due to their families having come from very distant places; a large permanent move, to the US, in their eyes could only have been for the best. The very best.

Chapter 13

Clapham, Part II
Cambridge-in-the-hills
and Schoolchildren

By September we were all settled back home in London, and our lives contained a schoolboy. Andy, now five, went to the local Macaulay Church of England school, which was much recommended. He filled the house singing, 'Raisin, raisin!', which we thought surely must mean 'praise him, praise him'. And the thing that came next was a best friend. Daniel Letts, whose family we befriended for the usual play dates and chauffeuring but who became real friends as well. John and Sarah Letts were a delightful, quiet couple of many talents. They lived in a beautiful, large Georgian house by Clapham Common. They had four children – Robert, Matthew, Daniel and Vanessa.

John started literary enterprises – the Folio Society and the Trollope Society – was involved in the National Railway Museum in York and the British Empire and Commonwealth Museum in Bristol. Sarah was an artist, an enamellist, who made and sold beautiful jewellery. Apart from her talents in the garden, she also co-wrote (and illustrated) a very good cookery book under her maiden name, Sarah O'Rorke. It seemed there was nothing she couldn't do: she was also a competent amateur recorder player. Sometimes we played in the same group. Our friendship (especially mine and Sarah's) lasted to the end. Although there were gaps when we moved, our friendship flourished again as widows. I treasure her cards and letters, as she didn't use the internet. She died unexpectedly in November 2017, in her sleep, and I am full of sadness and regret; I wish I had seen more of her. It was a huge shock for all who loved her, and even harder for her children.

In Clapham we were accumulating new friends. Among them were Connie and Nick Harman, who lived nearby with their two boys, but the marriage didn't last. Connie, however, remained her gregarious self and we met her at many parties and events. We had friends in common, especially John and Sheila Hale, with whom we were really close, and also Bamber and Christina Gascoigne. Jean Franco, who taught Latin American literature at Columbia University in New York, often came back to her flat in Clapham North when in England, and we saw as much of her as we could. She was English and a delightful jolly petite blonde, as vivacious as could be, and she and Eric could talk Latin America, and other subjects, ad infinitum.

No one could be more hospitable than Paul Wengraf, an art dealer from Vienna, and his wife Gertrude, whom everyone called Dada. They lived in Putney and opened their house to friends most Sunday afternoons. The Dial House, as it was called, had a circular garden and a small, charming pool. The atmosphere made everyone of all generations feel welcome and at home. The house was full of art – African art was their main focus and attraction. High tea was ready around four o'clock, or whenever we had finished making the sandwiches and laying things out. The number of people could range from eight to over twenty, including their children Peter, Tom and Monica. The house also had a splendid mynah bird called Clever, but one day, with the cage door left open, he flew away. As Paul became less mobile – by this time he was in his seventies – Eric usually went to talk to him by his chair in the sitting room. What did they talk about? I suppose art, Vienna, politics and so on. For both of them the time was always too short.

I don't like the expression 'earth mother', but Dada exuded these qualities, as she was open-minded, open-hearted, full of generosity and completely natural. I think she would have made a dreadful actress – there just was no pretence in her. She was good at *fun* though, and interested in everyone except possibly herself. Dada taught German at Morley College near Waterloo and lived to celebrate her delightful hundredth birthday party in style, organised by her children and grandchildren.

I was not a full-time mum. We had au pair girls – mostly they worked out well – although one was ghastly and one disappeared in the night. An Italian publisher of Eric's asked me to translate into English the letters Antonio Gramsci wrote to his children while he was a political prisoner in Italy. Gramsci was one of the founders of the Italian Communist Party. When sentencing him at a political trial in 1928, the prosecutor said, 'We must stop this brain from thinking.' Gramsci spent the next ten years in prison and various clinics. He died soon after his release in 1937 of a brain haemorrhage in Rome. The Gramsci story is a twentieth-century tragedy of the greatest proportions. I worked very hard on this task and it also provided some respite from hearing my children cry or quarrel downstairs. It was all going rather well, but it turned out someone else was also doing the very same thing – the publishers got it muddled – so I stopped. Actually, it was a bit of a relief. I didn't think Gramsci's letters were all that appropriate for his young children. He criticised too much and one was aware he had not been in children's company for a long while. He was very ill at the time and horribly treated in prison.

We usually went up to Wales during holidays, half terms and all of August. We were always surrounded by friends. I believe that without fail, all of these relationships stemmed from Cambridge. In fact, the whole area should have been called Cambridge-in-the-Hills. How anyone could read any books or do any studying in those undergraduate days there beats me. The Cambridge friendships started before my time, but once I got used to their loud speaking, I fitted in easily.

Already in the valley when we arrived were members of the Bennett family, Kay Herzog and her daughter Anne. The house was also used by relatives, including her sister Liz Eccleshare (daughter of Cambridge dons Joan and Stanley Bennett), who had known Eric since his under-graduate days. She came frequently with her husband Colin and their children.

Historians Edward Thompson and his wife Dorothy and family were neighbours in a farmhouse over the hill. They had many visitors (often historians from the USA), and people liked to say one could hear more typewriters clicking than birds chirping in our valley. I have fond memories of New Year's Eve parties at the Thompsons and that sobering, bracing walk in the early hours against howling winds to reach our car, a magical way to start the New Year.

Plas Brondanw, the home of the Williams-Ellises, was also in the Croesor Valley. Clough himself was at Cambridge, as was his son Kitto. His wife Amabel (née Strachey) was from a different background. She was a writer and a very lively intellectual, always keen to question and discuss many topics with Eric. Unfortunately she was an early riser and Eric was most certainly not. But he grew very fond of her. One April Fools Day, I invented her proximity in order to hurry him out of bed. One of the Williams-Ellis daughters, Susan, who married Euan Cooper-Willis, also educated at Cambridge, was a designer and together they formed and ran the well-known beautiful Portmeirion Pottery.

Needless to say we all visited and ate (rather well) at each other's houses. The middle classes know how to look after themselves, even though we went around in our oldest, moth-eaten clothes and throwaways from London. Eric's Cambridge friend Robin Gandy was enormously good company and invented postprandial games, often requiring one person in turn going out into the kitchen for five minutes (hopefully to begin clearing up). Robin, alas, had the longest laugh known to mankind. It went from pianissimo to fortissimo with much staccato too. Although it seemed funny in the countryside, it was much less so in a London cinema, as we discovered when reciprocating his hospitality.

Later on, Walter and Dorothy and their five children

joined the crowd and rented a very small picturesque gatehouse called Gatws, into which they all somehow squeezed.

The odd man out in this harmonious group was the artist Fred Uhlman, a Jewish emigré from Stuttgart, who was lucky that a friend had advised him to move to Paris in 1933 when Hitler became chancellor. Fred got by selling his paintings and drawings to private clients. In 1936, when Hitler became a dictator, Fred was able to cross the Channel to England. Still his luck continued. On a trip to Spain he found true love and met his future wife, Diana Croft. Unbeknown to him, she was a wealthy, top-drawer English aristocrat whose family home was Croft Castle (dating from the fourteenth century and now a National Trust property), halfway between Leominster and Ludlow, about an hour and a half's drive away from the Croesor Valley. Their marriage took place in London and although Diana's parents were dead set against it, particularly her father, the ultra-conservative Lord Croft, there was money to buy a large and beautiful house in Downshire Hill in Hampstead.

Together they became a good and caring couple. They started an artists' refugee committee for stranded Jews who had fled Germany and Austria, trying to find accommodation for them in England. The office was in their new home; I find newlyweds opening their doors for a charity very commendable. Diana's contribution was indispensible. They also founded the Free German League of Culture – while Hitler was attacking and closing down German culture, the League was set up to counteract and enhance it – which attracted many established artists and prominent intellectuals, including Oskar Kokoschka, Alfred Kerr,

John Heartfield, Kenneth Clark, Stefan Zweig and more. However, Albert Einstein refused his support, as he felt the project had been taken over by the far left.

Fred adored the North Wales countryside, including its strange industrial buildings, and after the war they went on holiday to Portmeirion. They struck up a friendship with Clough and Amabel. One day, walking with Clough in the Croesor Valley on the slope from Parc Farm, they came across an old disused cowshed behind which was a panorama stretching right down to the sea. Fred asked Clough if he would be able to design and enlarge the cowshed into a house to use as a retreat. Clough actually agreed and it became a spectacular modern home that blended with the land and was very much off the beaten track. Clough called the new home Beudy Newydd (New Cowshed), which he rented out to Fred on a ninety-nine-year lease. Ten years later, when we moved to Parc, the Uhlmans became our neighbours. But Diana felt she was neglecting her responsibilities at Croft Castle, and they came less and less, and passed the house to their son Francis. We were invited over by him and got to know him; nice guy.

We now had two schoolchildren. Julia started in the infants school in September 1969, and she was ready. Before she started school, when we went to collect Andy at the end of lessons, she would peer intensely through the school windows, working out where her classroom would be and where to hang her coat. I think on the day she finally started, she knew exactly where her peg was and rushed in. Other new children were clinging to mums, some were crying. Not our girl. I was the one that didn't know whether to laugh or cry.

Eric was away on his travels much of the time – I can't

say I felt settled in Clapham, which I should have been by now. I did try. We started to have some dinner parties – Francis Haskell came with his new bride Larissa, whom he had recently met in Leningrad and who was also an art historian. After supper, she asked us when the dancing would start. This question, among others, continued to charm us for years. For instance, she wanted to know how to survive Christmas in England when you had no car, no children and no television. That problem was immediately solved, as they both came to us for Christmas Day lunch for ever after. It became an established tradition.

Chomsky kept his promise to visit us, even though it was just a fleeting visit. I can see us all now, sitting on the stairs, and Eric explaining to the children about words. Andy asked Chomsky, 'Why do we call blue, blue and red, red? And not red blue and blue red?' 'Aha,' Chomsky replied. 'That's a very important question, and am not entirely sure I know the answer.'

I suppose my Clapham blues seriously began when Eric was in Paris. In May 1968 Eric had to attend a conference on Marx in Paris organised by the UN. He found the prepared papers extremely boring as usual, but what upset him profoundly was the fact that the delegates were impervious to the exciting student demonstrations going on outside in the streets. It was a remarkable time of infectious rebellion against capitalism, leading to the largest general strike in France. The anarchists wouldn't miss out of course; there was a fire and street battles in the Latin Quarter. The Marx delegates were holed up inside, completely missing the entire happenings. I daren't think what was in Eric's mind at this dramatic time. He must have been in silent despair. He wanted change so very badly, but instead the rebellion predictably fizzled out and the Marxist delegates would continue in their same old unbendable ways.

It was then that it struck me there was a jinx on us in that house or in Clapham, and we felt slightly gloomy. I had become a bit superstitious (must have picked that up in Italy). Maybe it was a simplistic way to explain away my strong intuition that we were not in the right place. Around that time, I had started to trust and follow my instincts more confidently than actual logistics. It seemed ridiculous that my mother and family all lived in north London while we were in south London. On the Sundays when Eric was writing, which was most of them, I drove the children right across the city to be with my family.

In reality I didn't have enough close neighbourly friendships. I do not believe women with young children can ever really flourish without this support. The people in the two next-door houses were invisible. We never, ever saw them. The people in the street opposite were in their Caribbean world and were out at work all day. Only on Sunday mornings, when they were cleaning their cars, did we exchange greetings. There was a dangerous main road between us too. That was how it was; our paths didn't cross. Eric was quite content in Clapham but I must have worn him down.

I began to realise that our domestic happiness was in my hands. I started vaguely looking, and one day I found a perfect house in a Hampstead street that led straight into Hampstead Heath and Parliament Hill.

Chapter 14
Our New House

The housing market in the seventies was beginning to boom. All the agents were going mad with gazumping and other legal but disreputable practices, and the estate agents Benham and Reeves were mocked as Benham and Thieves. It was jolly good luck that Mr and Mrs Forbes, owners of number 10 Nassington Road and whose house I was coveting, were old fashioned and sentimental. She insisted on selling to a family with children. They would not budge from that. I made the kids dress nicely with white socks, and brought them along to impress, and it worked. Mrs Forbes said she would save the house for us and she kept her word and kept to the original price. That's women doing business.

The house had three floors, a cellar, a small balcony, a decent-sized garden at the back and pretty flower beds in the front. The next year was all taken up with the move. A fair amount of work was needed, like taking out fireplaces, installing central heating, extending the kitchen and last, but by no means least, putting up bookshelves *everywhere*.

But it was certainly very much the house for us. It felt

right. Of course, it was not ready on time – which house is? Dorothy Wedderburn stoically came over on our first night there and we managed champagne on ice and something or other to eat. Also known as 'Doffy' (her baby pronunciation of Dorothy), she was one of Eric's close friends from Cambridge and their friendship lasted a lifetime (they died three weeks apart). She had joined the Communist Party while at Girton College in 1943 and stayed in the party until 1956. Although a member of the great and the good, she refused to accept an honour that was offered to her by the Queen. She always looked so grand and took good care of her appearance – in Eric's obituary of her, he recalled her eightieth birthday and how she had 'reserved a table for the staff of her Knightsbridge hairdressers'.

Moving to Nassington Road was a night to remember; Dorothy became a joint best friend that evening. There is so much hope in the air in a new house. Full of dreams and expectations.

Chapter 15
Home, Sweet Home

Our move from a main road in Clapham to Hampstead, NW3 felt like from polar ice to the Equator. Our house was halfway up Nassington Road towards the Heath. There was so much greenery around, I perceived our home as a country villa. We all loved it; I had not uprooted us for nothing. Eric and I remained there until death did us part.

By chance, Eric already knew our neighbour, Manny Tuckman, a retired GP, and his wife Gita, a sculptor. They ran an artist collective at No. 12. John Southgate, an impressive jazz pianist, was a tenant there who we were friends with – except on the nights he forgot the time and would play way past midnight. The first friend I made lived two doors down: Barbara Zeinau at No. 6 and her German husband Sigurd, a theoretical physicist. It didn't take long to get to know many other neighbours too, but Barbara and I bonded so easily. We are the same age and she was a teacher at St Dominic's, a local primary school. Some say we looked alike.

We have both moved away now, but to this day she still faithfully phones me every Sunday morning for our weekly chat. Sigurd died unexpectedly, and after raising her two children, Varina and Matthew, Barbara became the wife of a delightful architect. He was one of those boat people, restless on land, and was soon off sailing again. Barbara used to come over often, expecting Eric to be away too. During a sweltering heatwave, hot enough to stay outdoors, we talked all through the night in my garden, drinking wine and grumbling about our absent husbands, who were either sailing or lecturing. That long night cemented our friendship for good.

With so much travel and Eric often being away, home traditions were very important for us all. I am not one for surprises. I like to know what's coming and what to look forward to. Christmas is perfect for this; in fact, I ran it like a military operation. It was a Herculean task for me to keep the show on the road for three days, and then pack up for Wales on the fourth.

Christmas Eve (the continental Christmas) was reserved for the four of us only. We had a festive candlelit supper treat on our own for around thirty years – a tradition that all began in Nassington Road, and continues to this day. It was an immovable feast – while I did preparations in the afternoon, Eric would take the children to a museum (in the days when they stayed open on Christmas Eve) or the cinema. My own little ritual was listening to the Festival of Nine Lessons and Carols on the radio from King's College, Cambridge while I stuffed the turkey and scoured the ham to decorate with cloves, both large enough to last over Boxing Day. I enjoyed knowing that so many people would all be doing the same as me. There is a sense of belonging in shared tradition. Recently I heard our friend Hella Pick say on *Desert Island Discs* that

Die Kinder (Walter, Marlene and Victor) in Vienna

Marlene on the wall of her nursery school

My family in the garden in Manchester

Happy emigrés proud to be digging for victory

Marlene in Capri at the Arco Naturale

Eric in Marlene's Paddington Street flat during their early dating

Marlene posing with the United Nations welfare team in the Congo

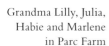

Grandma Lilly, Julia, Habie and Marlene in Parc Farm

Benedetta, Anna Rosa, Marlene, Eric and Rosario at the Villari's home in Cetona

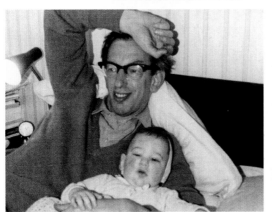

Eric bonding with our first born Andy

Babes in the woods (Milo and Eve)

Eric sharing a joke with the Queen

Roman, Anoushka, Max, Rachael and Wolfie

Eric with Milo, Eve, Wolfie, Anoushka and Roman at Julia and Alaric's home

Grandma Lilly's 80th birthday party; Isobel, Tanya holding Zac, Julia, Emily, Benjamin, Andy, Charlotte, Zoe, Habie, Grandma Lilly and Humphrey

Andy, Julia, Marlene and Eric

although she felt deeply about being British, 'I still wonder if anyone not born in this country is ever fully accepted and integrated.' My experience is different in that I feel totally integrated, accepted and loyal to Britain, but in my head I'm a Continental woman.

On Christmas Day, the house was a little more full. Grandma Lilly, cousin Gretl, plus a dog always came to us, as well as Francis and Larissa Haskell. Later we acquired the Italian historian and professor of Classics, Arnaldo Momigliano, who also joined the tradition. Eric fetched him and he always arrived, presenting me with a CD of music by the seventeenth-century Italian composer Gesualdo. As I enjoy predictability, this always gave me great pleasure. Sometimes the odd foreign scholar or two who had not reckoned with the British Library being closed and needed Christmas cheer came too. I am not sure how much our children enjoyed these rather intellectual Christmas Day lunches, although they became very fond of the Haskells.

For Boxing Day, Eric's communist friends came for a cold buffet, polishing off food from the past two days. Regulars were Margaret Heinemann, the archaeologist, Tamara Deutscher, the writer and Monty Johnstone, a writer and lecturer, among others – usually about fifteen people. It was totally casual - they were a loud, jolly lot and I'm sorry the names have gone from my memory now. The next day, we would pack up our things, and drive six hours to Wales, where we stayed until after New Year had rolled in.

Chapter 16
Academia

E ric's career had a marvellous and also lucky trajectory, although it began badly and very slowly. Like many Eric's progress was hampered by the Second World War, and for him it was further hindered by the Cold War. As a member of the Communist Party of Great Britain, he was automatically monitored by MI5, who took it upon themselves to hinder as many job possibilities as they could, and the press label 'Stalinist', which haunted him throughout his life, did not help.

Despite achieving a double-starred First from Cambridge, among other academic triumphs, he was still turned down from teaching positions at Oxford and Cambridge, which was disappointing and surprising for him. In 1945, his application for a full-time position in educational broadcasting at the BBC was vetoed by MI5, even though he was considered by the BBC 'a most suitable candidate'. A couple of years later, he finally secured a lecturing position in history at Birkbeck College, London.

The acting Master of Birkbeck, a medievalist, Professor Darlington had a personal antipathy towards Eric as well as disapproving of his politics and Communist Party membership. He was heard to have said that Hobsbawm's promotion from reader to professor would only take place over his dead body. As we know, life is stranger than fiction: Professor Darlington died very soon after uttering these words and when Ronald Tress became Master, he overruled the edict, much to the relief and delight of all the staff, who had been clamouring for this promotion for a long time (it was getting to be quasi-scandalous).

By the time he became a professor, Eric was already in his mid-fifties. Better late than never. But he never wasted his time bearing grudges; I tried to learn this from him, but I am still only a beginner. I remember buying a high-waisted Empire-line dress, as was the fashion, for the dinner celebrating his promotion. Our big academic journey had begun and we were on our way – the escalators were going upwards.

From time to time, Eric would tell me he wished he had studied anthropology. At school, he didn't know there was such a subject – his teachers had earmarked him for history. But he did it anyway. He was so interested in peasants and all those who cultivated the land, and his heroes were those who helped fight poverty and oppression: rebels like Robin Hood, and the Mexican revolutionaries Pancho Villa and Emiliano Zapata. I remember Eric talked to me about Quico Sabaté, a Spanish anarchist, and how he admired his bravery in the struggle against Franco and the Spanish state, so much that he had tears in his eyes as he told of Sabaté's killing.

Chapter 17

Sabbatical in Latin America en famille

Eric's passion for Latin America had been ongoing for about twenty years, so when he was offered a six-month sabbatical in 1971, he jumped at it. Firstly, it was a chance to improve his Spanish and secondly, it gave him the opportunity to continue his deeper research into peasants, their rebellions and above all, agrarian reform. Since Fidel Castro in Cuba had apparently shown the way for social revolution in the region, Eric was feeling politically upbeat. And of course he (and all of us) were elated over the failed 1961 American military invasion of the Bay of Pigs. Latin America was, as Eric described in his memoir, a continent 'bubbling with the lava of social revolutions'. But I regret to say that now, in the twenty-first century, we can see this didn't happen the way he had hoped. Though improvements there have been plenty.

Quite soon after moving into Nassington Road, we were preparing to travel. I was kept busy liaising with the teachers at Gospel Oak School, where the children had just nicely settled in. The head teacher, Ron Lendon, was very accommodating. Not only did he give permission for the children to go away, and held their places open in the school, he went above and beyond to keep the classmates in touch. Possibly too much – while in the La Sierra in Peru, Andy received thirty letters all saying exactly the same thing: 'We went to Camden Lock and took boats on the canal.'

Departure day arrived. We would travel to four countries: Mexico, Colombia, Peru and Ecuador. At all passport controls we held our breath. Not because of communism or visas this time, but at some point Julia had drawn a blue ship in my passport and it was too late to get a new one. Reactions were unpredictable – they veered from, 'Which child drew this?' in a friendly manner or disappearing with the passport to check with a higher official. A defaced passport is actually invalid, so very much was at stake.

Our trip began in Mexico City, but our luggage unfortunately did not. We had to travel via Lisbon, where it remained. It turned into a rather undignified April Fool's day arrival, extremely hot, and various academics were summoned to help us buy underwear and other essentials. When this situation lasted over a week, Eric lost his patience and announced that if our suitcases didn't arrive within two days, we were going straight back home. Then in the Latin American way, a VIP, presumably the ambassador, was contacted and, abracadabra, all our suitcases arrived the next morning.

We stayed with a charming French couple, Jacques and Lucero, who had a big house with grounds, and the children liked it very much. There were two dogs – a Dalmatian named Joreck and an Afghan hound named

Bingada, as well as two kittens. It was not all play for the children; every day they had some lessons with me, and Andy had to keep a daily diary-cum-scrapbook, which he did very well. I am using it now to write this. Lucero also gave each of them a daily painting lesson.

Ralph Miliband, who was also working in Mexico City, lived in the house with us. We were already friends with him and his wife Marion from London, but it was good to get to know him better in our new exotic surroundings. A warm and interesting man, and we were very glad to have his company.

He fitted so well with us – his children, David and Ed, were of similar ages to ours, and he was a sociologist and Marxist author.

We enjoyed exploring around the nearby Chapultepec Park with the children and we also went on many excursions including the Pyramid of the Sun (which according to Andy's diary had 750 steps, in case you wanted to know), the canals of Xochimilco, with their marvellous coloured gondolas, the city of Cuatla, and Lago de Patzcuaro, to name a few. We were within walking distance of the house where Trotsky had lived and was assassinated (now a museum).

We also went further afield to Cuernavaca, a beautiful city where Eric's friend Ivan Illich lived. We spent the day at his house as the children played and swam in his pool. Originally from Vienna, Ivan was a philosopher as well as a Roman Catholic priest, who wrote many books about 'deschooling', believing all education systems ruined our lives. He also wrote books including *The Powerless Church* and *Medical Nemesis: The Expropriation of Health*, among many others. All of them were ultra-controversial and people spoke of him as either a genius or a crackpot. Eric stood on the fence and referred to him as a European ideologue.

Downtown Mexico City there was also the marvellous and world-famous National Museum of Anthropology, which we were all crazy about. For the children it was so engaging and educational, with many replicas of the interiors of ancient indigenous (also referred to as 'Indian') homes. They were like big dolls' houses you could walk into. However, it was in the centre of the city, so it was difficult just to pop in with the children. The area we lived in, Chapultepec, was about fifty minutes away by a bus packed to the brim.

Lectures in Mexico were noisier than those I was used to. Young boys selling chewing gum from trays on straps round their necks loudly shouted, 'Chicklets! Chicklets!' throughout the talks. Eric was nervous at the beginning as his Spanish was rusty, but he mostly managed to cobble together something good. I remember seeing his name on a flyer in a lift, advertising a lecture of his in a vast auditorium the following evening, an event he knew absolutely nothing about. But Eric had learned to wear his flexible hat in Latin America. He was quite a little celebrity there. At this time in England, Eric was not well known and certainly not the intellectual public figure he would become, but in Latin America it was quite different – partly it was his interest in them and their lives.

Everything Eric wrote was translated into Spanish and Portuguese by his fantastic publishers, Critica, in Barcelona, Paz e Terra in Rio de Janeiro, and, later, the larger Companhia das Letras in São Paolo, Brazil.

We were fêted and invited for dinner often by the

many people Eric knew (friends, colleagues, pupils and ex-pupils). In Mexico, supper is indeed a night affair for the adults, and a lot of the talk revolved around politics. We were especially good friends with Carlos Fuentes, the well-known Mexican writer, and his wife Sylvia, who was a journalist. Leaping ahead in time, Eric reminisced in his last speech to friends on his ninety-fifth birthday in London about 'waiting for something to eat until almost midnight in Carlos Fuentes' house'. Our time here was soon up, and making our farewells to the warm and exuberant Mexicans was not an easy thing to do.

Two thousand miles and four hours on a plane later (according to Andy – our new trip adviser), we arrived in Bogotá, Colombia. Eric's friend Orlando collected us in a jeep. Eric had been commissioned to write a substantial piece for Bob Silvers in the *New York Review of Books* on the FARC. These were the Revolutionary Armed Forces of Colombia who were supported by the Colombian Communist Party, which had managed to survive the fierce internal conflicts of the 1960s. Eric was able to meet many of its leaders and supporters. With the World Wide Web several decades off, he had to surround himself with all the local newspapers he could seize.

We stayed in a very pleasant hotel in the centre of Bogotá, but I was worried about the children playing in the lifts and being mistaken for Americans – *gringos*. Much kidnapping was going on and I was on edge about it. Also, I wasn't quite sure how best to keep the children occupied. But as usual, Eric had contacts galore – luckily all his academic friends had maids in their households and help was always offered.

Bogotá's climate is usually rain or cloud, but to my amazement I learned that a one-hour car or train ride would take you to a sunny climate with blue skies and a marvellous swimming pool. Sometimes I was lent a maid to accompany us, or alternatively one of the wives who could speak English came, making a real holiday of it. In fact, all of Colombia was a holiday for me; plenty of time to daydream and think, as well as look around. I should have brought my copy of García Márquez's book *One Hundred Years of Solitude* to read again.

Apart from many prettily painted, colourful churches with friendly façades, the big attraction in Bogotá was the Gold Museum, which was astonishing. Andy was most taken by being inside the golden strongroom with the golden safe – he was already interested in big money. The museum had corridors paved with gold, like Dick Whittington's imaginary London streets. On the walls, glass cabinets displayed intriguing, mainly pre-Columbian objects, ornaments and jewellery – some primitive, some that one would love to wear today.

After my cushy weeks in Colombia, it was time for a more simple and rustic life in Peru. I expect Eric had not finished enough research for the Bob Silvers piece, but we had to fly off to Lima. I hope my readers are ready for a headful of agrarian reform, because this is the reason we went.

Here it was all about land: who owned it, who cultivated it and who was being exploited since the Spanish conquerors stole it way back in the sixteenth century. From the 1920s onwards, peasant revolts were brewing in Peru and getting stronger towards the late sixties. While we were there, a progressive military government (which sounds implausible, but really existed) under General Velasco Alvarado was in power. He predicted the peasant unrest intensifying and so his strategy was to hand back the large estate farms to the original indigenous owners, but under strict state control. Naturally there were conflicting opinions on this. I think in Eric's mind it was probably the best hope for Peru's impoverished peasants; he wrote in 1970, 'If ever a country needed, and needs, a revolution, it was this.'

These issues of expropriation inspired a group of brilliant young historians to form a research team. This included Joan Martinez Alier (a Spanish man's name, by the way, pronounced 'Huan'), who was then a research fellow at St Antony's College, Oxford, José Matos Mar, who was director of the Institute of Peruvian Studies, and the Peruvian historian Heraclio Bonilla, who came up with the idea that the papers from all the expropriated haciendas (farms) ought to be collected to form an agrarian archive at the University of San Marcos in Lima.

Pablo Macera, a distinguished historian at San Marcos and long-time friend of Eric's, was very much in favour of this scheme and he must have roped Eric in. With Eric's participation, the team got the blessing from the crucial Agrarian Tribunal.

The research team deliberated over the best place to go, and considered the sugar-cane plantations on the coast. But in the end they plumped for the more interesting pastoral and agricultural haciendas in La Sierra, the mountainous area that includes the Andes. So it was to be sheep. Well, we knew about those. But unlike Wales, it was not at all a serene pastoral scene. The Peruvian sheep could not safely graze. They were called *chuscas* in Spanish and *wakcha* (meaning orphan or poor) in the indigenous language of

Quechua. The *hacendados* (estate owners) wanted to get rid of the poor-quality sheep belonging to the indigenous shepherds, leading to continuous animosity and sometimes violence between them.

The plan was to start at Huancayo, the capital of the central highlands, where Joan discovered boxes of confidential letters dated from 1920 to the 1950s, before the telephone reached there – a prize for the archives, I should think. We travelled there by train, together with Joan, where the first-class passengers received a supply of oxygen if they needed it at the highest point – the Ticlio Pass, around nearly 5,000 metres (16,000 feet). Eric and Andy did suffer some *soroche* (altitude sickness), but it didn't affect Julia or me. However, I had my share of mosquito bites, which were huge, including one on my nipple, but they never touched Eric, always right next to me. (I ask you, is that fair?)

Huancayo is a lovely little commercial town surrounded by mountains. But we only stayed one night, as it was more convenient to be in La Sierra with everyone else. We stayed in a cottage. We met the British anthropologist Norman Long from Manchester University, who was living in another part of La Sierra called Matahuasi with his wife Ann, also an anthropologist, and their children Alison and Andrew. Visiting them entailed a fifty-mile journey on a bus with chickens, but my time with them was so special, I didn't mind. Ann and I would work on the children's lessons together, with even a bit of recorder tootling. At 'Sierra playtime' the children all fell on each other with joy; Andy wrote in his diary 'it was super playing with English children'. I felt he was sighing with huge relief. At some point the Longs very kindly looked after Andy and Julia for a whole day, allowing Joan, Eric and me to travel by taxi up to about 4,000 metres (13,000 feet) to look around a new, totally modernised hacienda called Laive.

The taxi driver drove like a demon and we couldn't stop him doing so – he thought it was funny. I was scared out of my wits for the sake of the children if we died. I couldn't breathe with the high altitude and anxiety. I gave Eric a look that embodied: 'Why are we here? Why did I marry you? This is too much.' I was having a wobbly. Thank goodness Joan always stayed calm and kind, because Eric did not.

We did in fact arrive safely. In the main building, there were important papers of value for the archives. We looked around the other buildings, where we saw into the white, pristine future – it was like being at a luxurious high-tech dairy farm. At Laive, the expropriation had been extreme. Much like the eighteenth-century Highland Clearances of the croft people from the Scottish Highlands and Islands, the cruelty was atrocious. The indigenous shepherds and their stock, such as lamas, were pushed out of their grounds. The new *hacendados* really needed more free land for their contemporary farming practices and above all wanted no contamination between the species. It was terribly cruel but necessary. Joan and his wife Verena went back to Laive at a later date to collect those papers, which they managed to pack and ship to Lima's Agrarian Archive. Joan later went to Cerro Antapongo on his own, among many other places in Peru, collecting papers for the archive.

Back in Lima, Eric's friend Pablo Macera seemed to take charge of our recreation at weekends. He was a man who didn't fit into any pigeonhole – very original, exuberant and domesticated. He was a great cook, but that meant enslaving everybody in the household to this purpose.

You can imagine the meals in huge casserole dishes, to which everybody could come – this was his way. Pablo became our leader, always taking charge of making our stay memorable. He was so delighted we had come and I think he temporarily 'expropriated' the university bus for our convenience at weekends. He then invited his family and friends, some servants and even some pets to travel around on the bus with us. We all sang songs together, including a Peruvian vowel song. I found this an ideal way to travel. This is how we saw the Peruvian countryside, stopping where and when we wanted along the way, sometimes chatting with strangers in restaurants or cafés. We didn't go especially to hear music, but there was so much of it around – at parties, in the open air, in the streets. And of course wooden flute music was prominent.

As a family we had already made our expedition to the old Inca capital Cusco and to Machu Picchu; Andy probably gained more out of these historical trips than six-year-old Julia. Like me as a child, I think she was very happy just spending so much time with her family. Here in Peru's Sierra, Eric was in his element. He was doing very much what he wanted. Surprised at feeling so at home in this faraway place, Eric was charmed that on the slopes of Machu Picchu he could find little wild strawberries (berry-picking is an obsession for anyone with a Mitteleuropean background). This is precisely the magic of Latin America, mixing touching European familiarity, with exciting foreign exotica.

Pablo arranged to take us all to a bullfight. I was interested and excited, but didn't enjoy it – I have never liked black humour and this seemed like black sport – however, I wasn't as upset as Pablo's four-year-old daughter, who for the entire time softly cried, '*Papa, por qué están matando a los toros?*' [Papa, why are they killing the bulls?] Papa took absolutely no notice of this repeated little plaint. It all lasted for what seemed ages. Nevertheless, Andy and Julia, as well as Pablo's son, were totally thrilled and mesmerised. Later Andy wrote about all the rules of this dangerous sporting ceremony in detail.

After a farewell dinner for all of us, it was our last time to say goodbye, and now we had to make our way home. We again had to fly via Lisbon, as the best connection was from Quito – the exquisite little capital of Ecuador. I think we only stayed three days. This was mainly to reconnect with people Eric knew – old students and friends – but also many new people who were apparently keen to meet us. Eric liked nothing better than getting information straight from the horse's mouth. We never did sightseeing alone like tourists, but were always accompanied by local people who showed us the best and knew what to miss out.

Ten miles to the north of Quito is the small town of Otavalo, inhabited by indigenous locals. We went there on a day visit and along the way we crossed the Equator, where the children had photos taken – Julia in the northern hemisphere, Andy in the southern. The 'Indians' all wore short, loose trousers, a black hat and a poncho. They each had one long black plait hanging down their back. They are famous for their handcrafted textiles – weaving, ponchos, tablecloths – and sell these goods around the world, where you can see them in Manhattan, Paris and so on. We were told it was cheaper to buy in the market in Quito, which you had to get up at 5 o'clock in the morning to visit – which we actually did (I bought hand-embroidered tablecloths for Mum and Gretl). One was expected to bargain, which

Eric loved, but I loathed. This is always my problem in developing countries. I bought a poncho and later saw the same one on Hampstead High Street.

Chapter 18
Bourgeois Life in the Seventies

S urely everyone is glad to be home, wherever you've been, after a long absence. Home is knowing where the tea bags are. I had a purpose again, organising the whole place and picking up where we left off. But I was easily overwhelmed at such times. My mother used to say she usually felt I had the water right up to my neck. I am afraid she was right.

Eric and the children nestled back into their familiar routines easily while I was dealing with new situations. Our overgrown garden sparked an interest in horticulture for the first time, although I was ignorant of plant names in English or Latin. So I began my own little agrarian reform, making the usual mistakes of planting big things in front of little ones. But I developed a complete new passion for growing old roses, especially French ones like 'Zephirine Drouin', 'Albéric Barbier' and, after my mother died, I planted a 'Louise Odier' near the house. The colours, names and smells intoxicated me. I automatically acquired a new subject of conversation, as it turned out that loads of people loved French roses too.

We also found ourselves with an adorable distraction, having somehow acquired a cat who insisted on belonging to us. She just waltzed into our lives one day and none of us wanted to part with her. We put a notice on a lamp post outside, but nobody claimed her. We decided on the name of Ticlio, after that highest pass in Peru, though when I had taken her to the vet it turned out she was a female and her permanent name became Ticlia. She was a most handsome tabby cat with four snow-white patches on her nose, chin, neck and paws. She had a good character and was not difficult – although she hated laughter, which was a hoot, and was easily annoyed by recorder playing. She knew Eric was the important one because he made the least fuss over her. Ticlia was loved by us all – she never got lost and was with us for fifteen years.

My life seemed to be at a watershed. My family continued their normal lives while I began to do things I'd never done before. I enrolled in an ILEA (Inner London Education Authority) recorder evening class where I met a set of completely new people. Our first teacher, Peter Wadland, was a delight, and extremely talented. His day job was running the Early Music repertoire for Decca Records. It was his ultra enthusiasm that got us going. He would actually jump up a little, saying, 'Yes, that's good. Please let me hear it again. One more time.' It was a long evening for me. Early shepherd's pie for the family, then a dash down to Marylebone Grammar School for the recorder class, over two hours of playing, and then off to the local pub. I did not want to miss out on the instalments of everyone's weekly updates. We made a very satisfactory group.

*

It was wonderful to see our dear friends again after half a year away. Several have already cropped up in previous chapters. As always, many stemmed from Cambridge. They were all sophisticated and could get along well with anyone. In our core circle were Gabriele and Noel Annan, Neal and Isabel Ascherson, Paul and Sally Barker, Leslie Bethell, Nick and Rosaleen Butler, Linda Colley and David Cannadine, Cynthia and Roderick Floud, Roy and Aisling Foster, Michael Frayn, Catherine and Erich Fried, Jack Goody, Richard and Vivien Gott, Felicity Guinness, John and Sheila Hale, Francis and Larissa Haskell, Bruce Hunter and Belinda Hollyer, Ian Hutchinson, Nicholas Jacobs, Martin Jacques, Helena Kennedy, Marina Lewycka, Brenda and John Maddox, Karl and Jane Miller, Juliet Mitchell, Gaia and Hugh Myddleton, Kathy Panama, Ruth Padel, Stuart and Anya Proffitt, Emma Rothschild, Garry and Ruth Runciman, Joseph and Anne Rykwert, Donald Sassoon, Graeme Segal, Stephen and Tia Sedley, Amartya Sen, Leina and André Schiffrin (when in London), Jean Seaton, Yolanda Sonnabend, Vanessa and Hugh Thomas, Claire Tomalin, Marina Warner, Dorothy Wedderburn and John Williams, Lindy and Robert Erskine.

Just looking at this list makes me smile. This is the core group we drew from, but it was interspersed with others all the time, often depending on who was in London.

In the seventies, dinner parties were the norm, usually with eight to ten at the table. Cookery books, especially Elizabeth David, were all the rage. I spent a lot of the time on the telephone, organising who would fit well together. I would think nothing of phoning Jack Goody in India, where he could easily be, if not answering his phone in

Cambridge. Eric would have liked the dinners to take place once a month, but then he only saw to the wine. Gradually, towards the naughty nineties, it became more popular to throw larger parties for more people, which were sometimes catered for professionally. I suppose as we grew older, we all made more and more friends.

At our dinner table, we wanted to talk without noise or muzak: conversation is all. If the ambience is right – informal, casual – then people are relaxed enough for freer talk and might come out with things they've never said before or thoughts they are still formulating. In any case, there was much chatter among the chattering classes on whatever was current – I liked it best when one conversation was happening around the table. The food was as *casalingo* as possible. No posh things *en gelée* or shaped food en cocotte, just simple, familiar and plentiful dishes, mainly dependent on the weather. Three courses was the usual custom. In the seventies guests still expected cheese or savoury after puddings, but was eventually phased out.

Sometimes I made food that could be laid out for a buffet and people helped themselves. It's nice for guests to get up, and in England everyone feels comfortable queuing. I remember a dinner party when, completely out of character, I said, 'Oh, now we're older we seem to talk more about food; we used to talk about sex.' Gaby's response was: 'Well, Marlene, think of the varieties. Take spaghetti alone … alle vongole, al pomodoro, all'amatriciana, al'arrabiata, bolognese …'

I am no longer sure when the children stopped wanting to play host, mingle and hand out olives to the guests; I suspect Julia (who was more gregarious) enjoyed it for longer than Andy. As they entered their teenage years, their interests were beginning to shift. Julia was spending her time with friends but still singing in the school choir. Andy began learning the guitar and often had an expression on his face that seemed to say, 'Hey, why am I not skateboarding in California?' No longer little children and not yet adults, they were coming into their own.

At some point, Clough Williams-Ellis had decided to restore and refurbish the 16th c farmhouse of Parc Farm. It was part of a larger farm complex consisting of a grand manor house, two big barns and a beautiful small pond beside the farmhouse. It was just about a mile down the Croesor Valley from our cottage Bryn Hyfryd. Waiting for the restoration to finish, it would be two years before we could move into this larger and more romantic house called Parc. Clough had left a tree growing out of an attic room. By now it was so tall, Eric had an extra clause inserted into our lease in case it toppled over in a storm (all of this to the dismay of our lawyer). It was not a cosy home, but we fought the damp and slowly adapted. It had so much character and style. We were still in Snowdonia National Park, and as before, still going on our usual, wonderful walks as well as discovering new ones.

After the commotion of moving house on a fine sunny day, I caught a glimpse of Andy and Samantha Campbell-Jones going for a walk hand in hand. This was a big surprise for me, but their innocence was so sweet. When the children were younger, Eric and I agreed that he would deal with religion and I would deal with sex – but when the time came with Andy, I felt it was Eric's territory and I wanted him to have a hand-on-shoulder chat (even though on this occasion it wasn't necessary). Samantha was one of two lovely daughters of a charming family who were great friends of Dorothy and Walter and often spent their holidays in the Croesor Valley.

We were now a few metres away from Dorothy and Walter, who had moved in to the gatehouse of Parc Farm. Their youngest child, Zac, used to sit outside, where Eric was kept busy chopping much-needed wood for our damp indoors. Many conversations would take place between Eric and the toddler. Once, when Zac repeated something to his dad, Walter asked, 'Who told you that?' to which Zac replied, 'The woodcutter!' pointing towards Eric.

The farmer, Dai Williams, looked after vast numbers of sheep, but no longer any other animals. Whenever coming into conversation with him, Eric would end up unconsciously speaking in a Welsh accent for a while. He had a habit of doing this; the same would happen speaking to the local garage owner, or asking 'Where ya from?' of a New York taxi driver. I didn't mind, but it was entertaining to see how embarrassed the children were. Quite often we three had a good laugh at Eric's droll and eccentric character.

I remember a fine summer weekend when our friends Amartya Sen, the economist, and his wife Eva Colorni came to stay. Eva was for many years my closest friend. She was an Italian economist and teacher, as well as a very domestic and intimate person. She was totally involved with her family and children, Indrani and Kabir. Her death from cancer, when the children were young, was the most shocking thing in my life. Even though Eva was my best friend, I did give Cupid a very small hand in helping Amartya get together with his new wife, Emma Rothschild. I felt Emma was the best thing for him, and the children. In the end, their happiness is what Eva would have wanted most. And so it proved to be.

Before we knew it, both our children were desperate to start life and the 'awkward teenage' years were now upon us. Andy was ambiguous about staying on at school, and continuing with more exams. We were not tiger parents and we never wanted to push them; as Andy recalled, 'I remember that Dad was so keen for us not to feel pressure of following in his footsteps,' but for fear of doing this 'he put no pressure on us at all to go to university'. Clearly, we had taken our eyes off the ball. Eric and I felt higher education could be delayed until later in life if necessary, but we insisted they must at all costs get their A levels.

Eric took the initiative and decided to send a lost and muddled Andy to a sixth-form college called Bransons, split between a first year in Canada near Montreal and a second year back in the UK in Ipswich, which did wonders. He really wanted to go to Canada and their outdoors programme seemed very enticing for him. He came home a confident young man with three A levels under his belt and with many friends of both genders. I remember my mother being very impressed that Eric had put all his principles against private education aside and did what he felt was right for his son. Upon reflection, it could have been in part his original school, William Ellis, who overdid their disappointment that the 'son of Eric Hobsbawm' was falling short of their academic expectations. Andy recently admitted that 'if someone had said to me that university is a unique opportunity for learning and forming memorable life experiences and making lifelong friends, I might have considered it differently'Julia was different: she did want to go to university, but somehow did very badly in her A levels and did not get anything like the required grades to read English literature at Sussex University. This was an enormous shock to her. She was very disappointed indeed, but on reflection she felt that during school she had been intellectually underrated by her teachers, who deterred her from applying to prestigious institutions. Julia admitted this dented her confidence and caused her to 'stop trying a bit' with her A levels.

Instead she attended the Polytechnic of Central London to read Italian and French, but never enjoyed it. Among other reasons, she found herself surrounded by mature students while she herself was only seventeen. She decided not to continue and began working at the student union, where she fell in love with the union president, Alaric Bamping. Andy remembers feeling both concerned and impressed at receiving letters from Julia while he was travelling. She wrote about student protests organised by Alaric (was there perhaps a resemblance to her daddy?), where everyone barricaded themselves into the student union building for days on end. So, the older brother was looking out for his little sister, just like my brother Victor did for me.

Chapter 19
Martin's 'At Homes'

While we were in Latin America, our friend the architect Martin Frishman and his mother had been planning to move to NW3 to a large house in Chalk Farm, which had a huge studio for Martin's collection. It had belonged to Vanessa Redgrave, who had never lived there – it was left to her in a will. By coincidence, they moved in 1971 when we returned, but Martin's dear mother Margaret died a year later.

It was after her death when Martin began his very special 'at homes' for his large circle of friends. These were wonderful evenings, each with their own unique cachet. Mostly his guests were composers, visual artists and writers, including Alice and Georg Eisler, who lived in Vienna but visited London often, Thea Musgrave, Peter de Francia, Elias Canetti, Erich Fried, Catherine Boswell, Max Neufeld, Yolanda Sonnabend and friends, Kathy Panama, Amalia Algueria, Jacob Lind, Frederick Sampson, Lalo and Viviana Fain-Binda, Susie Barry, Estela Weldon and Alexander Goehr. These are the ones I can name now. All were pretty left wing, and in this highbrow artistic and intellectual milieu

Eric fitted like a glove. More than that, I like to think he was one of the attractions. They could talk about politics, opera, music, literature and visual arts into the night; to me it seemed they had all read everything. I was hungry to absorb it.

As you entered the house and made your way towards Martin's studio, huge posters of ships, locomotives and trains assailed you. He didn't distinguish between highbrow or lowbrow – you might find an exquisite painting or etching in between two posters of 1930s steamers. Martin's studio was filled with objects from around the world and a big blue rowing boat hung from the ceiling. I think his heart was really all for travelling, observing and bringing the world into his home. He was an unusual collector.

His main passion at that time, however, was Islamic archi-tecture – he had become an expert. Sometimes he showed us the slides he brought home and needed for his teaching at the Royal College of Art, the Architectural Association, and at UCL, which was blissful for Eric, as he was himself crazy about Asian art in general, and Japanese, Chinese and Indian specifically.

The guest list varied, but Martin was a great host and cook, if somewhat ambitious. So these evenings were definitely not to be missed. Martin was a bachelor, with no shortage of girlfriends, but he had to be patient to find his number one. After ten years, his true love appeared, an Argentinian architect of Italian origin, Federica Varoli Piazza. As Martin had been our best man, Eric returned the honour and was best man at their wedding, and then a few years later I was the driver to the Royal Free maternity department when their beautiful baby daughter was on her way into the world. She was named Greta after her paternal grandmother.

Chapter 20
My Music Career

M y path to becoming a music teacher was by no
means ordinary, and I would describe it as a mix
of determination, sheer luck and the right people at the
right time.

I knew my first step was to become a member of the
Society of Recorder Players (SRP), which has branches in
most UK cities. Everyone who can read music and play the
recorder is welcome; conducted by professional volunteers,
we would sight-read all afternoon.

I enrolled in the Marylebone SRP, a very lucky branch
run by Theo Wyatt as chairman and musical director. No
one more witty and knowledgeable would ever be found.
Theo also ran many other courses off his own bat, each
one with a distinctive agenda. His most ambitious course
took place over a week every summer near the sea, outside
Drogheda in Ireland. The sessions went on all day and
were inclusive of all levels, ranging from brilliant (who
might even be professionals already) to competent, to those
who sometimes lost their place. Grouped by ability into
one-to-a-part quartets and quintets, it must have been an

enormous task to curate the music, especially before technology as we know it.

The venue was a large, comfortable house and in the seventies we could safely leave our instruments and belongings in unlocked rooms. The sea was less than a ten-minute walk away, close enough for a quick dip in between music sessions. Our communal evening ensembles were hugely enjoyable, and sometimes the more professional players delighted us with a performance of their own. There were also lessons in ceilidh dancing – I remember my partner once being a nun! There were often nuns there, who enhanced the music by playing their fiddles. One didn't sleep very much but it was worth it for the fun we had. I treasure the memories of such a variety of new music, beginning to understand the Irish, making new friends and the many gems Theo would come out with while conducting, such as, 'Speed in music kills just as much as it does on the motorway.'

Back in London, I was enjoying my evening classes at the ILEA (now led by Nancy Winkelman), but I discovered that the one-week residential courses were far and away the biggest help and stimulus for me. There was a new one coming up that I was really interested in, and some of my group (Bob Horsley, Alistair Read, Annie Pegler and Terry Over) had already booked in. It was months away, but I planned to go with them to Herefordshire. Now that Julia and Andy were older, I felt Eric would cope. Also, these residential courses always took place during the relaxed holiday times – relieving Eric of juggling the practicalities of term times.

This course was the jackpot for me. While it offered a variety of areas for study, it was not at the top of my agenda to concentrate on my own performance and virtuosity at this time. My mind was elsewhere – I wanted to work with children. I liked introducing music to them. There was indeed a daily session on teaching recorder in schools, and it was here I found my true calling. I was delighted it was run by the musical director of the mid-Hertfordshire SRP, Herbert Hersom, and I already knew his pull was towards recorder learning at primary level.

Herbert had much fine music up his sleeve and introduced us to beautiful compositions for beginners that included only three to five notes. Here we had our very own English composer, Colin Hand, starting with his *Come and Play Books 1* and *2*. To me they seem like *Lieder* without words for young children. The titles of the pieces are evocative enough and tell you all you need – 'Waltz', 'Swinging', 'Sailing', 'Fanfare', 'Echo Song' – with delightful piano accompaniments.

On this course I picked up even more tips and insider knowledge over meals and during our free time, as we all talked shop non-stop. No one listened to the news, and the outside world didn't exist. I found amateur musicians were on the whole extremely amiable, modest and jovial people – quite a different species from academics. Coming home was always fantastic. The children were beside themselves with excitement and eager to talk without pausing, even though we were only apart six days. Alone together over supper that evening, Eric sensed this shift in me and suggested that before committing to deeper education in music college (which I was about to investigate), I should consider getting a teaching job, 'Why not see if you like it first?' He was convinced that I knew how to play the recorder well enough to teach in primary school, and he knew my flair with children. I took his comments to heart and I got in contact with the head teacher, Terry Seaton, of the nearby Carlton Junior School. He was ambitious for his school and eager to introduce instrumental music there.

I felt good vibes. Terry made it obvious that he wanted me to join his school. He was straightforward with me and I recall him saying most awkwardly, 'I am not concerned about you not being a good fit for this school, but that you may be shocked or upset by some of the things that come out of the mouths of the children here.' I reassured him that I was a woman of the world and could handle what was coming my way (maybe I should have said I was not a lah-di-dah lady and my husband was a communist.)

As this was my first teaching job, my position would be part-time in the school, with part-time training. I was to have an audition at the music centre in Pimlico and later an inspection whilst teaching the children at Carlton. So Eric was right to steer me this way. It worked out even better than I imagined because it offered plenty of training.

I had already heard along the grapevine that the new head of music for the ILEA, John Stevens (later Sir John Stevens) was a very enlightened man. When hiring music teachers, he was less interested in people with long strings of letters after their names but keen on those with an interest in child development (excellent news for me). It seemed clear he had a vision to lift music in schools out of the Stone Age. He wanted to expand the music curriculum for all children in all his schools and I was eager to learn this new *class music* – a method that encouraged teaching in a group outside the classroom, in a space where children could move and form a large circle. It focused on learning through musical games, movement, imagination and variations of sound through listening, and also handling instruments. Stevens had certainly picked incredible teachers for our training, they were brilliant, all of them – Leonora Davies, Diana Thompson, Wendy Bird and Stephen Maw spring to mind. It was not just their extensive knowledge of material, but the way they handled the instruments with care and poise was contagious; a bongo would not be banged on but cradled like a newborn and then gently tapped with fingers. Oliver James was the recorder specialist for the ILEA. While I can't recall the exact pieces I played at my audition in Pimlico, I remember it going well. Oliver's inspection at Carlton School took nearly half a term to materialise and so I had time for preparation. Looking around the music shops, I found the recorder section invariably on the lowest possible shelf next to the floor. Tutor books for all other instruments seemed dignified, with a one-to-one tutorial appeal. Although the recorder is often taught in large groups, I could not see why books for beginners had to reflect a classroom cacophony with jokey faces and silly characters. So I made up my own sheets for teaching at Carlton. Later on, I wrote two tutor books for beginners, *Me and My Recorder,* which Faber Music published in 1989. They were well received (and also translated into Greek) and I am happy to say they are all in print today and am still getting respectable royalties. My daydream now is for a Chinese edition.

In the class inspection, Oliver James had really come mainly to see my interaction with the children, and the ambience I created with and around them. The eight- to nine-year-olds were especially drawn to songs with stories in them, like spirituals once sung by slaves in America. The ten- to eleven-year-olds played a samba, which

Oliver noticed I had renamed 'Please Miss, Can We Play the Samba?'. I was certainly learning the importance of repertoire.

I loved my time at Carlton, teaching three mornings a week. Slowly over the years, recorder playing blossomed. A natural progression of trebles and tenors were introduced and Terry the head teacher even bought a bass recorder. Performances, alas, were frequent, but still made me anxious. It took me a while to learn to stay cool. There were many concerts and we appeared in the local newspaper as the Carlton Academy. Eric often made an appearance and got used to sitting on the infant chairs. Some days I wondered if I didn't learn more from those children than they learned from me. Their spontaneity, honesty and inquisitiveness were a constant reminder of life's essentials.

After my ten years there, the junior school was forced to merge with the infant school, creating chaos and tension for children and teachers alike. Sensing this, Terry asked, 'What can I do to entice you to stay, Marlene?' To which, with astonishing confidence, I replied, 'I need an accompanist. I'd like you to hire my friend Don Randall.' I'd met Don in a recorder group. He had retired from a tough boys' secondary school where he had been doing all the music for forty years. A musician through and through, he was the perfect person for the job. He was hired – thank you, Terry. Don was so helpful and useful: it was bliss for me. The children liked him very much, and they respected this small, wrinkly man because they knew quality without realising it. Don was also my 'top and tail' teacher (helping a pupil who was either struggling to keep up or was way above average). So I carried on, and my job at Carlton School lasted another four years – fourteen years in all.

During this time, I was becoming more in demand, as was the status of the recorder. For instance, Angela Mendis, head of music at Fleet School, was helping to run the Saturday-morning 'Young Music Makers' and she asked me to take a group of children and adults. It was good fun because the children outshone the adults so easily and loved being taught alongside them. I had also been teaching one day a week for ten years at a private boys' school, Hereward House. This was a completely different experience. The principal, Leonie Sampson, was so supportive and generous; it definitely raised the level of my work.

I became more ambitious. The recorder players were learning an arrangement of Papageno's song from the opera *The Magic Flute* and I discovered a boy with an overwhelmingly marvellous voice. I started teaching him Papageno's words and although he was a shy child, lacking in confidence, he surprised himself and agreed to sing it at the concert. I rearranged the recorder part as an accompaniment with piano. His parents were delighted and bought him a costume covered in feathers of such splendour that not even the Royal Opera House could beat it. On the night, Papageno acted and sang his heart out. It was a complete and total triumph – I bless him, Mrs Samson and Mozart.

When I finally decided to leave Carlton, I got my last job at Beckford School in West Hampstead. I was in my late fifties now and decided it was time for a change. I taught there once a week for six years. Musically it was a lively school, with many different instrumental teachers coming and going (strings especially, Suzuki violin and cello). I picked up tips from the Suzuki teacher Jane O'Connor, whose pupils presented themselves so finely. Jane Hills, who became the head, was a recorder player herself. She even played in assembly with the children. This was a huge boost for the recorder's standing and reputation with the children and the parents.

I remember a very talented pupil there, nine-year-old Felicity Squire, who wanted to be a music teacher (her mother was a teacher and also a pianist). I recommended to her parents that Felicity attend a Saturday-morning recorder class run by Angela Rodriguez in Muswell Hill. Angela recognised her talent too and from there she moved on to CYM (Centre for Young Musicians) in Pimlico, where she had the excellent teacher Sue Klein. Finally she made it to Trinity College of Music with Philip Thorby, professor and director of Early Music, where she took her degree. She became a recorder player and music teacher herself. She was also a flautist. Bravo, Felicity.

All this music and all this time and I have not yet mentioned my friend Diane Jamieson, who helped me in my music career more than I can say. She was a natural and also an expert, full of imagination as well as experience. She was a genius on the subject I found the hardest: class music – aka controlling thirty children at one time, with drums and tambourines and more on the loose. Although I had by now substantial class-music material with successful activities, I still sometimes had wobbles on a Sunday night. I would go around to hers, and she would give me a song that would wow the Monday class into obedience and awe.

After my six years were over at Beckford School, I had ideas flowing in and out of my head about making music in another way. I remember it was now or never to embark on a completely new venture of my own: the After-School Recorder Players. I ran it at our home in Nassington Road for both children and parents, and our downstairs furniture was rearranged every Monday. Eric was remarkably flexible – in fact, he now knew how to put up a music stand and fold it back down. There were two groups, beginners, and secondly an ensemble including bass, trebles and tenors. I ran this programme for ten years until our travels abroad became too frequent and our grandchildren would soon be on the way. I roped Don in as pianist and also 'top and tail' teacher, enticing him with dinner and a lift home. I hired Felicity, who came straight to us from her lessons at Trinity College, imparting the latest wisdom and techniques from Philip Thorby, the maestro. By this time, Felicity was already a first-class musician – how luxurious is that for the north London parents to see their treasures making such strides under this direction? Felicity's rapport with the children was a delight to observe. Don was so happy to be involved in this project; he said with frustration, 'My only problem is that none of my friends believe me that every Monday evening I have dinner with Eric Hobsbawm.' Those two got on like a house on fire.

For our concerts, I normally hired a church hall or another suitable venue, but a few times the stage was our hall, with the audience sitting on the staircase. The project as a whole was an original and successful enterprise that ran entirely on word of mouth. I can't deny the pleasure it brought me.

Chapter 21
Manhattan

After Eric's retirement from Birkbeck, New York suddenly became a big part of our lives. The New School for Social Research, and the Graduate Faculty of Political and Social Science there, invited Eric to come and teach for a semester a year, starting in 1984, which carried on for twelve years. Unlike an ordinary university, the New School was on a mission to recruit well-known scholars. In fact, the Graduate Faculty started up in 1933 as the University in Exile in order to rescue academic refugees from Hitler's Germany. How very prescient and smart, as well as kind. Moving ahead to our time, they knew British professors had to retire when they reached sixty-five, and that is when Eric was approached. It was on the initiative of the dean, Ira Katznelson, which quickly won assent from his colleagues. Others were invited from France, Germany and the UK, including Perry Anderson. Some became full-time faculty members; others, like Eric, were invited for one semester each year.

Eric was very excited about the combination of heterodoxy, progressiveness and internationalism at the Graduate

Faculty, along with the able students it attracted from all over, including the USA, Latin America, Europe, Russia and China. Eric once counted twenty nationalities in his class. He immediately involved himself in the project of the New School and the role he played in it. I knew he would go above and beyond in his contributions to its agenda, and during the times I was not there, I felt sure his academic and social life coalesced even more strongly.

I really wanted to go with Eric for his first term and I organised wonderful substitutes for my recorder classes. The young and very talented teacher Angela Rodriguez took over at Carlton and my friend Emma Murphy, who was the best recorder performer in Britain at that time, took over at Hereward House School.

Now in their twenties, Andy and Julia were capable of taking on responsibilities and looking after the house while we were away. At the very beginning (for a month or so), Walter's eldest daughter Habie also lived in Nassington Road, until she moved to live with her grandma. Both children had jobs now. Julia was working in television, having zigzagged her way through the ranks in publishing, despite not having a degree. She then worked at Thames Television, which led to a research job at the BBC on the *Wogan* programme. She then moved on to a small, independent production company making programmes for the fledgling TV company BSkyB.

After spending sixteen months travelling in Australia and California, Andy returned to London. He was working in a combination of advertising sales and music journalism for London's *Alternative Magazine* – writing a provocative weekly column under the pseudonym Hamish

Head – alongside forming a rock band called Tin Gods. Alas, Andy's brief encounter with the recorder was inevitably replaced by the guitar. Both our children visited New York while we were there; in fact, on one of Andy's trips he was on board one of the first ever Virgin Atlantic flights in 1984, where he remembers the unusual experience of 'buskers with guitars playing music up and down the aisle'.

Eric and I arrived in Manhattan for the Fall term in September, together with other newcomers from US universities, Chicago in particular. These colleagues were Charles and Louise Tilly, Ary and Vera Zolberg, and even our dean, Ira Katznelson and his wife Debbie, who had come a little earlier. They all quickly became our friends and we explored Manhattan together, each contributing their new bit of knowledge of a good restaurant, or new brunch place, or where to buy bread from a different country every day.

Eric and I decided we would immediately have a most wonderful time, exploring Lower Manhattan especially, and every visit Eric insisted on his ritual of taking the Staten Island Ferry. We went a few times to the opera, especially for our anniversary in October. I remember seeing Strauss's *Salome* for the first time (you can't say you liked watching this revolting story, but you can't say you didn't, either), as well as a traditional *Don Giovanni*, which we never stopped enjoying, however many times we saw it. During our second visit, Bob Silvers (editor of the *New York Review of Books*) kindly gave us his stalls seats for the performance of *Rosenkavalier,* as he and his partner were both indisposed. In turn we gave away our balcony tickets to two students. It was conducted by Carlos Kleiber, with singers Felicity Lott and Anne Sofie von Otter, and it was an electrifying performance. We came out high as kites – neither of us could sleep until dawn. The orchestral players were drawn from all over the world and legend has it that Carlos Kleiber was the strictest of conductors as regards to the number of obligatory rehearsals.) But it was not all classical music, we went to many jazz clubs, and Eric's love of tap dancing brought us to see Jimmy Slyde – the best tap dancer known in New York at that time.

Our first apartment was around the corner from the New School on 9th Street, on the twelfth floor, with a view of the intact Twin Towers. There were an unusual amount of pink mirrors around the place, windows you could see out of but not into – it was like a movie. This extreme backdrop was perfect for wine and cheese parties. We knew so many people because of Eric's global contacts (many of whom found themselves in New York at the same time – you never know who you're going to run into on 5th Avenue). Luckily, my autumn visits always coincided with the charming Thanksgiving parties that dear Eric Foner, the historian, and his wife Lynn gave in their apartment.

I was never short of friends myself. One of these was Leina Schiffrin, my long-standing very close friend from England who moved to New York. Leina is a one-off – gregarious and always speaks her mind if she feels it is the truth. Perhaps her education at the progressive coeducational boarding school Dartington Hall played a role in shaping her free spirit. Her husband André was one of Eric's regular publishers (and an exceptionally good one). They were known for their Sunday brunches out on their penthouse terrace. Leina was up to professional standards in the kitchen and also gave the most delicious and convivial dinner parties, to which, invariably, interesting people came. Not just publishers and writers, but also artists, actors and UN people – André seemed to know everyone in town.

Another dear friend was Betsy Dworkin, whose husband Ronnie spent much of his spare time writing, not unlike my husband. We'd do special things together – she was originally a New Yorker and knew all the best spots – like going to exotic tearooms and walking along the river from Chambers Street to Battery Park, punctuated by small parks of different character. We also liked going shopping (clothes, of course), which in New York is surprisingly relaxing. It's much more lively, with the ease of refunds and exchanges. They know how to do business.

As the spouse of a professor at the New School I had the privilege of being able to enrol in any class that took my fancy, almost for free. Taking advantage of this, I started off with a yoga class, learning new methods with a stylish young teacher, and also dipped my toe into t'ai chi. Of the latter, I still remember being alarmed by the teacher, with his American accent, saying, 'When you do this posture, your ovaries are saying thank you.' It was OK – I was fifty-two years old.

I also took an art-history class, which wasn't free but well worth it. It was called 'Exploring Museums', and we toured the most famous ones, starting with the Metropolitan, Cooper Hewitt, the New-York Historical Society and ending with the Guggenheim. I don't often enjoy reading about the visual arts as written by connoisseurs (who mostly seem to explain how knowledgeable they are in order to impress other art historians), but our teacher Leslie Yudell was crystal clear and very engaging – she helped teach us how to focus and *look*.

The unit where my classes were held was in the original New School for Social Research, which was founded in 1919 for adults to study without any formal entrance requirements. Again I thought, how enlightened that sounds, and as so often in New York, years ahead of their time. I was thrilled to learn that Martha Graham taught dance there in the 1920s and Aaron Copland taught music, among other luminaries.

All I can say is that the time flew by, and Halloween came upon us fast. One cannot get away from it and nor did we want to. There was the big parade, with half of New York migrating from all over the city to Lower Manhattan. The handmade costumes that developed from the numerous art and design schools were fantastically impressive – I remember a skeleton dancing, made bone by bone with intricate detail. Eric and I only bothered with masks. We were very fond of that night, and although there was so much crime and violence in Manhattan, ironically it was always suspended at Halloween.

Slowly I was beginning to see the ups and downs of the city. Both tiring and exciting, the pace of the city never stopped and it felt like always being at a party. Nobody was shy, and strangers would come up and talk to you: 'Hey! I like your sweater, where'd you get it?' Quiet time for myself in public was always interrupted. Even though the children were adults, I still needed time to myself to think and worry over them.

I remember being appalled at the homeless situation, where many could be found living in the subway. There was also a huge area they had chosen to occupy in the deeper east area of Downtown. I have never seen such a thing before, even on television. It all seemed so strange;

they didn't appear to wear their sorrow on their sleeves, and the chaos of living on the streets looked structured and supervised, which in fact it was – it was part of the city's programme designed for the homeless. Homeless people often wanted to talk; I felt their loneliness. It was as if they had missed a train, the way you have to wait with despair for another, except this limbo was for ever.

Through Leina's network of friends, I met Inea Engler, who introduced me to the musical household of Lucille Wolff in the West Village – a huge pleasure for me. Luckily, musicians always need rehearsals and audiences, and I was made very welcome at 11 West Street, with its bohemian atmosphere and beautiful young players. I was in my element. In fact, I shall never be able to hear the Andante from Bach's Double Violin Concerto without emotion and the memory of Lucille's daughters playing it. People would often stop on the pavement below the windows to hear this *Hausmusik*. I was so happy to be able to walk there and back in such serenity for my own *soul*, away from politics and institutions.

Eric did get a lot of satisfaction from the students he taught, and learned from them in return, Latin American students particularly. They enjoyed each other's company as well. He was also pleased to be invited to the Institute for the Humanities at NYU every Friday to listen to special speakers, after which they all went for lunch. It was nearby at the Deutsches Haus in Washington Square. Altogether, it was a tremendous semester.

I would continue to come with Eric each year, but only for two-week periods during school holidays. Over the years, we began to feel at home with our lives, schedules and routines. We'd become New Yorkers. While Julia

enjoyed many visits to the city and had her own friendship circle and business connections, Andy actually moved
to New York for business in January 1995, working in a
pioneering internet start-up he co-founded called Internet
Publishing (which turned into Online Magic and later
Agency.com) and began dating Kate Ellis on Valentine's
Day that same year.

Chapter 22
Our Italy

M any of the highlights in my life happened in Italy: in Rome, in Capri, in Tuscany, in Venice, around the Neapolitan coast and in Milan. You will already know I lived there as a young woman, but Eric also had many past visits and experiences separate from mine. Two different Italian histories were already in place, but now it was going to be our Italy.

In November 1979, Eric and his historian friend Rosario Villari were both invited to the same conference in Venice. Eric was keen I should come, so I phoned Rosario's wife Anna Rosa, whom I had met recently to ask if she was also coming; she agreed to travel provided that I did also. We were all put in the same hotel (a nice one). November weather, often foggy, turned itself into a week of warm sunny Riviera temperatures. Unfortunately the husbands were disappointed in their conference; aside from having to take a fifteen-minute boat ride every day to the island of San Giorgio where it was held, they had grumbles about the organisation and the papers not being up to scratch.

We ladies, on the other hand, had one of our best holidays. We seemed to have so much in common, and I don't only mean that both our historians were paid-up members of the awkward squad. We were compatible –like sisters, and treated each other so. We picnicked on steps, bridges, in quiet, secluded areas away from the tourists. We once found ourselves near the famous orphanage where Vivaldi composed, gave violin lessons and also taught the girls to sing. The most talented ones would become members of the renowned Ospedale della Pietà orchestra and choir, which often toured around Italy and abroad. Not only Vivaldi, but Sammartini was also from Venice, and we probably had a picnic around his plaque too. Famous for being an oboist, he also played the flute and recorder (which was the norm at that time). He was a wonderful composer for the recorder and I have played and taught many of his lovely sonatas and trio sonatas.

Rosario, who was taking many years to write his main book, *Un Sogna di Liberta,* which covers the Neapolitan Revolution in 1647, really needed to get on with it and research in the British Library. We invited him to come to us whenever he wanted, and he did. That is when our deep friendship began. He was a marvellous guest and when joined by Anna Rosa it was even better. They were practical people, unlike the Hobsbawms. They knew how to fix things with tools – though Rosario always complained about Eric's being blunt and rusty. We all laughed that it sometimes felt as though we had hired them as a working couple. They even entertained us, as Rosario played French and Neapolitan songs (by heart) on the piano and sometimes Anna Rosa sang them. In the kitchen she was a wizard. It seems that two husbands and two wives in a household together works like a dream (why is there not more of this, I wonder?).

When Eric and I travelled abroad it was very practical for them to be in the house alone, not least for feeding and caressing Ticlia, and again Rosario went off every morning to the library. It took a few more years, but he did eventually finish his book in 2001 and it was very well received and reviewed. But the Villaris were addicted to London and this arrangement continued. Their home was in Rome, but each year they spent their holidays in their Tuscan farmhouse Santa Fortunata, beautifully situated and furnished (even with a pool, so they could rent the place out to well-off Americans). It was near the small town of Cetona. Later, our Andy and Kate stayed there as part of their Italian honeymoon, and Julia and Alaric spent time there for peace and quiet, during Julia's pregnancy with Roman.

We had many holidays there, just the four of us. We got on so well – the historians always had much to talk about, but it wasn't all chat about the dreadful politics (we were there when Berlusconi was re-elected). The kitchen, with the patio door to the garden and pool, was the centre of the house. So much time was spent there, and we enjoyed watching a one-act *opera buffa* unfold. The two protagonists were Pia and Rolando. Pia (soprano) was the maid (who secretly was still in love with her ex-husband Nilo, who ran the main restaurant and gossip hub in the town piazza). She came to work every morning and also cooked our lunch. The gardener Rolando (tenor) was in charge of the grounds that circled the entire property. He looked after the olive trees surrounding the swimming pool and the expansive olive-tree orchard behind; the garden also had pear, plum and two big fig trees, and he was in charge of growing all the lovely produce – courgettes, aubergines, tomatoes and peppers – and also watering the plants, starting with blue agapanthus at the front. The Italian sun makes these flowers much taller and more imposing than they are in England. Hostas are giants there.

Rolando was so attentive with the Villaris, but it was especially sweet and humorous to watch him be attentive to the provocatively dressed Pia, who he clearly had eyes for. Pia must have known, and she teased him by running outside when it suited her, complaining loudly, 'Dove sono i pomodori?' (Where are the tomatoes?). He would scurry off to bring them to the kitchen where he would then dawdle, always inventing something to fix. That was the comedy performed at Santa Fortunata every summer morning, except Sundays. Cetona was adorable; I think only the Italians can make piazzas like this. There were no cars, children played safely and there was a communal effort between mothers to watch over the others as well as their own if they stepped into a shop. Of course, we knew everything that was happening behind closed doors in Cetona (thanks to our Pia).

Anna Rosa and I continue to travel back and forth to visit each other, and our beautiful friendship continues today, but without Eric or Rosario, except in most conversation. Because of the the Villaris, we had masses of friends in Italy: theirs and ours – journalist Antonio Polito, historians Corrado Vivanti and his wife Anna, the Perrinis, the Procaccis, Beppe Vacca, the director of the Gramsci Institute, Toni and Giovanella Armellini, and too many more to name. We were also friends with Enzo Crea (a publisher of art books and poetry) as well as a professional photographer. He took the picture of me and Eric at La Foce on the back cover of this book. Benedetta Origo, was also a close friend who often invited us to her two beautiful homes, La Foce or Castel Guliano, in the midst of a glorious landscape of rolling hills and long distance panoramas.

From the beginning of the 1970s, Eric was very popular in Italy, but his peak was in the 1990s onwards. The Italians couldn't get enough of his books, which were all translated into Italian. Eric was first published by Laterza (*The Age of Capital)* and later Giulio Einaudi, a son of Luigi Einaudi who used to be President of the Republic of Italy. Because of this, Giulio was a very grand person and ran a very grand publishing house. Eric was much involved in Giulio's huge project *La Storia del Marxismo,* working as a principal editor (alongside Vivanti, Haupt, Ragionieri, Marek and Strada, among others) to find British scholars to be approached to write for it. His book on jazz (as well as *Captain Swing)* was published by Editori Riuniti, the Communist Party's publishing house.

Eric's next main publisher was Rizzoli (run by Paolo Zanino) and the publicist in charge Anna Drugman was the most competent and attentive lady, who made sure we were treated as VIPs every step of the way. In May 1995, they brought out *The Age of Extremes*, which was a huge success and presented at the big book fair, Il Salone del Libro in Turin, where he was also given an honorary degree at the University of Turin. I didn't go with him to this but managed to go to the next one, a literary festival in Mantova. I remember the charm of Mantova, and the adorable Giorgio Armani shoes I bought there.

Eric also got prizes, including the Premio Bari. We were invited to the premiere of a new production of the opera *Fidelio* at La Scala in Milan. The audience was full of stars, luminaries and, unlike in Britain, politicians were there as well – in the royal box was the former President of Italy, who was booed, and his party immediately left the building. In front of us sat Jeremy Irons and his wife Sinéad Cusack. Riccardo Muti was the conductor, and he was marvellous, as was the entire evening. During the interval, I overheard gossip in the ladies' room about Riccardo Muti's current lovers, which made meeting him at the big dinner afterwards – let's say . . . interesting. Eric was often approached at book fairs and other events by Italian politicians and friends, who would ask if he would write for this or that journal. He was enamoured with the way communism was actually developing in Italy, and how he was able to contribute to the political climate intellectually. Eurocommunism, as it was called, was appealing for Eric as it was softer and wanted more independence from the Soviet Union. This shift started in Prague and also became popular in Spain. Without delving into dialectical Marxism, Eurocommunism arrived rather lukewarm to the Communist Party in Britain, although it's true they did actually publicly condemn the Soviet intervention in Czechoslovakia. Of course, the Communist Party was not important to most people in Britain, and I was always surprised at the lack of awareness at just how active the Communist Party actually was in Italy and other parts of the West. Even in India it was not uncommon to find people wearing small hammer-and-sickle brooches.

When we were back in London, Martin Jacques asked

Eric to write for his magazine *Marxism Today*. The successful collaboration of many years led to a long-lasting close family friendship as well. Martin's son Ravi and our grandson Roman continue their good friendship.

Chapter 23
Mature Lives

In the 1990s, Eric and I were not yet old, but enjoying the advantages of maturity, or so *we* thought. We were at the peak of our abilities and consequently very busy. Our Welsh holidays continued, as we saw our friends and enjoyed the usual outdoor life. Walking was still very good, but getting over stiles was becoming a little challenging for Eric now. A more pressing issue was the rise of Welsh nationalism. It was starting to grow and we didn't like it. Some cottages were even burned down. The five-hour drive from London seemed less appealing. Betsy Dworkin recommended that we make contact with her friends Brenda and John Maddox, who had their second home in the Wye Valley near Hay-on-Wye, to get a feel for the area. We already knew John, who used to be in one of Clough's cottages, but since his second marriage to the Massachusetts-born writer, they had moved to a picturesque large farmhouse near Crickadarn. John was the editor of *Nature* magazine and Brenda was a biographer, journalist, critic, reviewer, novelist: a real lady of letters. I believe she went to school with Betsy Dworkin, where the

connection began. It would continue with the Maddoxes
and the Hobsbawms and their children – and eventually
grandchildren too. The Hay Festival made a big difference
to the area; they were used to foreigners from all over the
world and welcomed them with open arms. Eric's agent,
Bruce Hunter, had just negotiated a very good deal on the
advance for his proposed new book *The Age of Extremes*.
We were now in a position to buy a place. It was all very
new and exciting for us. About a couple of miles from the
Maddox farmhouse in a small hamlet called Gwenddwr
(pronounced 'Gwenda'), albeit with its own Anglican
church and also an independent Welsh chapel, we found
a totally rebuilt and refurbished cottage that looked as
though it had been patiently waiting for us. It was named
Hollybush and was also built from a ruin, but otherwise
it was the diametric opposite of Parc. Listen to this: it
had central heating, was newly rewired, the windows
would close and it had views nearly as far as England. The
house was as cosy as an apartment in Manhattan, though
surrounded by sheep. It also had a big garden wrapping
around the house and I was able to plant climbing roses.
Gaby Annan introduced me to a French rose called 'Papa
Meilland'; it was a velvety, deep red, regal rose that didn't
fade or wither until it turned black and was ready to die.
It was too grand for the cottage but I loved it and it was
much commented on in the village. Dorothy Wedderburn,
who often came with us, planted a plum tree and there was
already a holly bush with the largest red berries, in case the
house was used at Christmas. Another difference now was
the addition of Louise Nicholson, who came as a cleaner
but was essential in so many other ways. For second-
homers like us, who come and go, and have people staying

when we're not there, you have to have a friend like her. She would prepare for our arrival and take care of things after we left, which made it a real holiday – for all of us. She helped at our parties, she knew everybody and she mingled with charm and ease. Our move to Gwenddwr meant a different style of country living – no more going about in motheaten throwaways from London. The town of Hay became full of stylish garments. The general atmosphere is friendly and content in Wales, especially in Brecon, where we did our food shopping. It seemed as though all the women who worked in the supermarket were happy to be there. The Welsh like talking a lot, and here they could chatter all day long, because they knew the customers and had grown up with many of them. Also, the children behave well in Wales. They obey their parents, who are not on their mobiles all the time. The only thing that gets under my skin in Wales is their bureaucracy, which is dire. They love rules and regulations and go overboard in making them. There's nothing like recycling for inspiration – 'the super-handy scrunch test': if you scrunch it and it doesn't spring back, then it can be recycled. I recall a detailed instruction about comic books being OK, but then pondered if the *Radio Times* would also be. Walking in the Wye Valley is much easier here than in North Wales. The landscape is softer, so one can walk down the roads and lanes as well as crossing muddy fields. One would happily stroll around in a summer dress and pop in casually to visit friends. Chickens and hens run freely in the village. The annual agricultural show in each parish at the end of July is the big event of the year, and Gwenddwr was no exception. Nearly everyone participates in judging the best cakes, ponies, vegetable arrangements and even babies.

The year Eric was president, our granddaughter Eve won the 'best baby under six months' prize. We hoped people would regard it as the coincidence it was, and not that the London Mafia had moved in. As the English second-homers were mostly intellectuals, their house guests usually were too. It was a lovely mix of people who came to the show and you would be as likely to see Melvyn Bragg as the local farmer. Of course the *main* attraction in these parts is the Hay Festival itself in May. The local second-homer grandees were useful to the director, Peter Florence. John Maddox was made president of the Festival, then Lord Bingham, then Eric, who was succeeded by Stephen Fry (in my time). Peter Florence and Eric admired each other and spent time talking politics and the world. I'm sure Latin America featured. Maybe out of that came Peter's idea to expand the festival, starting with Latin America and eventually many other parts of the world. Eric was hugely popular and always filled the largest tent to capacity. After his death, Peter started a memorial lecture series after him, featuring big names like Joan Bakewell, Amartya Sen and the US politician Bernie Sanders. All this VIP speaking meant I had VIP entry (all the widows of ex-presidents are treated very well) and now I would need it. There is a lot of queuing up at Hay. And not everyone can rest up in the green room like us. I enjoyed being surrounded by friendly people living in Gwenddwr, especially, when I used to come alone, dealing with house affairs. Opposite us was the builder and electrician Idris and his brother Trevor, a shepherd. Next door, there was Marjorie and her dogs, who I would join for walks. She recently started a little open-air shop selling home-made cakes, flans, scones and eggs, which is a great addition to the village. Then there was Verona Atkins, a widow who was born in Gwenddwr, a charming lady with many interesting tales to tell about Gwenddwr's past. Next came Frank and Pam Banks, who were both teachers locally. Frank later became a professor of education at the Open University until his retirement. Now he is a churchwarden and chief bell ringer, and they live there permanently. Frank is very enterprising in starting up theatrical ventures and organising productions. He makes sure there is plenty happening in this quiet corner of the world.

Second-homers George and Phil Littlejohn, who live in Islington, became our close friends. A very joyful and social couple with lots of vivacity who love walking, theatre and anything interesting going on. They are such wonderful hosts, and we were usually there for a New Year's Eve party from which we could stumble home easily. Further down the road in Crickadarn is Jane Birt, separated now from John Birt of the BBC. Jane and I are so close, because she lives in London too but also visits Crickadarn a lot (with her large family). She lives next to Tony and Sarah Thomas, who are also close and hospitable friends. We've had so many memorable dinners there. Sarah is a viola player and Tony is a retired writer and journalist. Eric was a great birdwatcher and he and Dorothy would sometimes go off with their binoculars on excursions to do serious sitting by a lake for long stretches of time. I would drive them there and back. I didn't have the time to sit, and there were already so many birds to see and listen to on our ordinary walks. Every day when I could hear buzzards mewing I would look up and see them soaring high with their flat wings. The area was very well known for kites, and there were many organised opportunities to spot them, but we just kept a really good lookout and it felt like a goal to see one. But it wasn't all staring up at the sky. Eric also wrote a lot in Gwenddwr. He loved working in his study, which was so light, with two windows, each with a different aspect. I was also scribbling. I had been interviewing my housebound mother for a few months and was writing up the memories to make a book for the family. It came out in 1998, with wonderful photos, and I called it *Conversations with Lilly*. It was not a difficult book to write, but it was so convenient having Eric nearby to answer any questions – as Roy Foster said once, 'Eric was a world wide web in and of himself.' This quality made Eric very popular with young female students and many tried to flirt with him. But mostly I called it 'Ph.D. love'. You could almost see their thoughts forming: 'If I was with this guy, imagine how my Ph.D. would turn out.' At one time we found it so agreeable there that we toyed with using Nassington Road as the secondary home. But there was too much happening in London for us to miss. Our two children were now in their thirties. It was around this time they found out they had a half-sibling; without warning, Marion had told Joss's brother Joel, and so we had no option but to tell them about Joss, as we did not want them finding out accidentally. Although it was a big shock for them, they did bond as siblings very soon after. I also got on well with Joss, as we could talk shop – he was a drama teacher. As both our children had partners now, it felt like the right time to tell them. Julia had stuck with her student flame Alaric, and Andy with his New York Valentine. Maybe they didn't find their way to university, but certainly found (and kept) something more important: true love. Andy and Kate's wedding took place at the National

Liberal Club by the Thames. It all went off as beautifully and as stylishly as a wedding is dreamt to be. Strawberries and champagne were served on the terrace afterwards, followed by a hired double-decker red bus (destination: 'All Stops To Bliss') to take the guests to the apartment of one of Andy's two best men, Eamon, for the reception and dinner. The building was grandiose and ornate – once the headquarters of the state-owned British Gas. The evening finished with fireworks. The following day, I gave a lunch party in the garden at Nassington Road, luckily on a beautiful day. Some of Kate's relatives had come from Massachusetts and other faraway places and I wanted to welcome them. Four years later, Julia and Alaric decided to tie the knot at Marylebone Register Office. Two of their three children were also there; six-year-old Roman, wearing his first suit, and three-year-old Anoushka, who insisted on climbing onto Julia's lap during the signing. Wolfie was still a twinkle in his father's eye. Alaric's two children, Rachael, aged fourteen, and Max, aged twelve, from his previous partnership with Lesley Campbell were also there, and other members of both families. All helped to fill the large Cinnamon Club, which was chosen for its ability to accommodate their large guest list, which also included many babies and small children. It was such an amazing atmosphere, with the most witty and genuine speeches; much was expected of Eric, as the father of the bride, and he delivered. The Villaris were staying with us at the time, so they were there as well. The wedding programme read: '21 years after they first got together, 7 years after they got back together again, they are getting married.' Their romance was odd at the beginning, not least because of the ten-year age difference between them, but romance is romance, and after a decade of separation they were reunited. Both our newlyweds lived within a mile of each other and we were all close in north London. The family had started growing. I had already discovered that the first-born grandchild feels like being seventeen and falling in love again. If I had worn one of those medical twenty-four-hour heart monitors when Roman was being brought to me, the doctor might well have asked, 'Whatever happened to you at two o'clock? Your heart rate jumped off the charts.' Roman, being our first grandchild, rejuvenated us both. Two years later we found ourselves driving through ice and snow from Hollybush on New Year's Eve as Anoushka had decided to come into the world nine days early. We waited with anticipation and passed the time in a Greek restaurant with our friend and neighbour Liz Eccleshare. The baby was so tiny I thought the name Anoushka was too big for her, but now that she is eighteen it suits her perfectly.

One year after Kate and Andy's wedding, Kate's parents Jane and Bill Ellis flew over to London from New York for another confinement. This time it was very slow. We were all getting anxious about the very long labour, but when we saw him the next day, Milo was as cool as a cucumber and he has stayed that way throughout his childhood. Two years later, there was another arrival expected for Andy and Kate. To my delight I was asked my opinion on names. I was very thrilled and even more so when my choice was the winner. Eve, sometimes called Evie, looked more like an Ellis than a Hobsbawm – hurray! For Julia's third birth, I looked after Roman and Anoushka for the day. Because Roman wanted the new sibling to be a boy, Anoushka did too. They were adamant that it could not be a girl. Well, when I got to the hospital, there was a big, beautiful baby boy. Wolfie (Wolfgang) was the last grandchild to arrive. It was clearly time to roll up our sleeves again. We spent many Sundays together and for Eric the children were unbelievable. He never dwelt on his many years alone, but I know he neither forgot them. Sometimes he still found it difficult to believe that all these beautiful children running around the garden were his family. As a grandfather, Eric was quite a natural with little humans. And jumping ahead, even more impressive with teenagers.

Chapter 24
Age of Glory Travels

When we spent time abroad, we didn't feet like tourists because we were invited guests and Eric was so well connected with the universities, the academic world, journalists and publishers. Our travels began in modest hotels or student lodgings, which we thought would always be the way. Eric loved travelling and academic conferences were a good way of seeing the world. It seemed he knew remarkable people in every city and loved getting his information about the world from his foreign friends. Wherever we went there would invariably appear an old friend, often a historian, who would show us the real local life and tell us truthfully what was going on in their country. Travelling was such a big part of our lives and it's hard to put into words how much fun we had together because Eric was such an enthusiast. Whether it was packed cities or secluded mountains, little rivers or dense forests, the whole of geography was his passion. He never lost interest. With far too many places to name, I've chosen a selection for variety, but also because of the people and our connections that made those places so necessary.

Our trips around Europe were frequent and we had become accustomed to the Continent. Paris had both the familiarity of home and also the buzz of being new and thrilling. Berlin always resonated with me as we spent so much time with German emigré friends in England and of course for Eric, it was part of him. Orphaned at fourteen, he eventually moved to England to live with relatives. A bookish teenager, he joined the student Communist Party while Hitler was coming to power, distributing Marxist leaflets around his area. Being caught doing this would be instant torture and death, but for him there was no choice: you were either red or brown. Prague felt familiar, perhaps because of my background. Could it be the trams, the architecture, the way the streets were cobbled? An added bonus for me was the amount of marvellous recorder music available there. It's a very popular instrument in schools – and beyond – in Germany, Hungary, the Czech Republic, Austria and other countries in Eastern Europe. It was a super place for me to browse in music shops selling sheet music at risible prices. Not to mention how beautiful the cities are with their endless churches, which we loved strolling through together. Because of the short distance, it wasn't uncommon for a friend like Georg Eisler to come and join us from Vienna for a couple of nights.

Gradually our travels became different. People wanted a lecture from Eric, rather than his participation alongside others in a conference. If people wanted him, they knew I would have to be invited too. I measured this upward trajectory by the distance of our hotel to the city's opera house. It was getting nearer and nearer. This was particularly true in Vienna where I could look out of our window in Hotel Sacher Wien and actually see some opera dancers practising next door. Eric had been invited to receive the keys to the city of Vienna, a gesture we thought might (or might not) be connected to some public show for the appreciation of Jews. This nudged the University of Vienna to give him an honorary degree. I was born in Vienna and had two close cousins, Betsy and Patricia Higgins, who had gone back to live there from America and married Austrians after the war. For these ceremonies, I was always asked if I wanted to invite any guests, and indeed I did – I invited Betsy and Patricia for everything and they loved all of it. My cousins are such darlings and made time to take me to all the places of my childhood that I wanted to revisit. I also had plenty of time to myself to daydream in the city, thinking of Orson Welles and Alida Valli in *The Third Man,* and enjoyed it so much.

While I am talking about Austria, we were invited to the Salzburg Festival several times for Eric to give a talk on culture. As the years passed and Austria was turning right again, it sometimes made us feel really worried and guilty to be there, but we couldn't resist those operas, orchestras, singers, acoustics – there was no such thing as a bad seat. Then during the interval, you see people walking around in dirndls and national costumes and you begin to wonder who is a Nazi and who is not. It was tricky; we did not like Austria as such in these times, but I must say we had very good friends living there.

Another golden oldie was long-time friend Ernst Wangerman, a historian with a brilliant mind, with whom one could have such good conversations about the twentieth century, and his Spanish wife Maria Josefa. We had many wonderful outings with them, spending hours at the Austrian lakes. We would then go back to their house for supper, hoping Maria's marvellous gazpachos were on the menu.

Japan, where we travelled in 1990, was a category of its own. It was totally different in culture from anywhere I had encountered before. I would stay away from Japanese university deans if I were you – their stiffness was so marked. But when you were friends, and they had taken you to a nice familiar place, they behaved quite differently. They had to treat me as though I was a man because it was not customary for women to go and socialise with men in this way, and they didn't know how to treat me otherwise. With a little sake, they relaxed even more and they would tell you ridiculous stories and laugh freely. I often puzzled at whether they were embarrassed or just very jolly.

Eric had a great friend, a Japanese historian, Hiroshi Mizuta, who often came to London, sometimes with his wife Tamae. I'm sure he was responsible for our trip to Japan. Unfortunately his English was not getting better, but rather the contrary. Like all Japanese, he laughed a lot. He has just celebrated his ninety-ninth birthday this year and still corresponds with me from the university care home for elderly academics, where he lives. He has just sent me the Japanese translation of *The Age of Extremes*, which he oversaw.

I had two completely different trips to India. After Eric retired from Birkbeck, he treated us to a tour of India. Eric had been many times, but for me it was a first. Eric was enthralled by Indian art, which he knew quite a bit about, and wanted me to experience the country with him – no conferences, no lectures, no speeches, no responsibilities, just us with a nice group of strangers going sight-seeing. The tour was my introduction to the country and was beautifully arranged. We were treated so well everywhere. The Indians must be the friendliest people in the world. The only complaint would be the pace – the tour chose too many places to visit in the very short space of two weeks.

My second trip was different because Eric was invited to give talks and we were VIPs, not tourists. India is a tremendously hospitable country and they liked nothing better than to celebrate a prestigious scholar, and the nice thing was that they were scholars themselves. Eric had friends and former students there, and had had an attachment to the country since his Cambridge days. Manmohan Singh himself, prime minister from 2004 to 2014, was a student that Eric had supervised. And finally we could visit our super-scholar dear Romila Thapar in her own home and surroundings. That was a treat; we usually only met at conferences. We also saw our friend Premja, who had spent a month deciding which restaurants would be good enough to bring us to when we came. Luckily he comes often to London. I admired the middle-class academic Indian women, so efficient at organising their lives: they were scholars themselves, perfect hosts, and beautiful-looking with their colourful saris and elaborate jewellery. They did it all. I know they had servants, but all the same, they were remarkable with their vibrant energy.

I'm trying to remember my first trip to Brazil in the 1980s. I was in my mid-fifties and we travelled to Rio de Janeiro. Eric had been invited to speak at a conference after *The Age of Empire* was recently published. Eric's first publisher in Brazil, Fernando Gasparian, who ran Paz e Terra, insisted we stay in his house surrounded by the most beautiful botanicals. I remember it as a light, palatial home with a dining area and a long table for over twenty-five people. Everything was so spacious, and the family's hospitality boundless. They invited many people to see us – the lyrics of 'The Coffee Song' should have been 'There's an awful lot of kissing in Brazil'. We met Fernando's wife Dalva, who was full of warmth and joy, and their children Helena (studying to be a diplomat), Marcus (who now runs Paz e Terra) Laura and Eduardo. Helena was put in charge of being our chauffeur and guide, and what lovely company she was. It was perfectly clear how highly Fernando thought of Eric; he was always planning new projects and places to see, informing us that we would go by private plane! He was so excited to have us there and seemed to want the whole of Brazil to meet us. I knew Helena and Laura would be coming to London – how would I repay this kind of hospitality? But they were friends, and it was easy.

Another journey to Brazil was ten years later, for the launch of *The Age of Extremes* published by Luiz Schwarcz of Companhia das Letras in São Paulo. Luiz organised the entire trip. He turned out to be an unusually generous, sensitive person, which is quite rare on this planet. He and his wife Lili looked after us warmly in the bosom of their family in São Paulo. When we first arrived, we managed to get time alone, just the two of us, before all the activity began. I think it was near Paraty, where we stayed at a charming hotel and with a beautiful little pool just for a few days. Then we were ready for the launch, the press, the lunches, the speeches.

Luiz had to take us to Brasília, where it was arranged we would meet President Fernando Henrique Cardoso and a very splendid Brazilian presidential lunch took place. Eric knew him well, but as the women and the men were casually separated, I didn't get to know him. We had a brief amount of time to see the ultra-modern architecture of the city, designed by Oscar Niemeyer and Lúcio Costa, before the next part of the schedule brought us to Rio de Janeiro, where the book would be presented. So here we were again, walking along the great beach of Ipanema, home of the 'The Girl From Ipanema'. Eric did love Brazilian music – the fusion of jazz and bossa nova was very much his thing.

It was on this trip that I saw the favelas. I wondered how people survived in these shantytowns, with the crime especially. By this time, I was ready to go home and for the launch to wrap up successfully without any incidents. My recollection of the book launch is that it filled the 1,000-capacity hall but many still were unable to get tickets. It was organised by Maria Eduarda, of the cultural arm of the newspaper *O Globo*. Sometime later she became the partner of our great friend Leslie Bethell.

Eric had become something of a celebrity in Brazil. Leslie later recalled flamboyant fans shouting, 'Eriky! Eriky!' down the streets at the 2003 International Literary Festival in Paraty, where he and Eric shared a platform. Some women even asked for kisses – '*Dê-me um beijo!*' – and they wanted to be photographed with him.

This really was the age of glory for Eric. He was awarded so many honorary degrees as well as prizes. One of the most rewarding was the Order of Companions of Honour, which was given to him by the Queen in 1998. Eric was delighted and proud. It was very special for him. As before in his life, it did not involve a rejection of his politics.

However, his old friend Dorothy Thompson refused to speak to him indefinitely for accepting this honour. Strong feelings on all sides.

Other awards included the Ernst Bloch Prize, Bochum Historians' Award and the Balzan Prize. The Balzan was one of the most prestigious and his wasn't necessarily given unanimously. It was contentious to give it to a communist. Unfortunately Eric had caught a virus and was unable to collect it from the House of Parliament in Bern in Switzerland. This caused consternation and the Swiss insisted a helicopter, no less, be sent to Hampstead Heath for him. In the end Julia collected the prize and gave his speech undaunted, as she is.

I used to worry about this new success and eminence. Once I remember having to deal with paparazzi. Might it go to his head? Would he still be the offbeat professor from Birkbeck, known as the 'historian from below', famous for championing the poor and dispossessed? But through all the honours and awards, he didn't seem to become any more vain than other successful academics. Although Eric didn't quite hold on to all his resolute beliefs, he still thought that the point of life was to try and make the world a better place.

Now frailer and in his nineties, Eric's last trip would be to a part of the world we'd never visited before. This invitation to Doha, Qatar came nicely, as it also fell on our forty-eighth wedding anniversary. The Egyptian author Ahdaf Soueif, in collaboration with Bloomsbury Publishing, wanted to publish a book on the brand new Museum of Islamic Art, designed by I. M. Pei and opened in 2008. It was built on the end of an artificial peninsula, surrounded by water with intense sun gleaming on it. A fusion of the modern and ancient, it was really a magical place. They invited a wide group of intellectuals and asked them to write on one aspect of the museum for the book. It could be on anything: a painting, an object, the architecture or just the atmosphere itself – the writers were given free rein. Bloomsbury published the book beautifully, but in his very old age Eric's behaviour had at times become too spontaneous and he gave our copy to a lady guest who was admiring it in our drawing room. I was furious with him for a long time. Alas, I don't expect Bloomsbury have any copies left. Needless to say, everything in our visit was first class, or higher, if there is such a thing – the flight, the hotel, the food. Morning, noon and evening there was a constant buffet from all countries with staff attending at all hours. We had such exciting company, nothing but intellectuals in a happy mood, stuffed with good food and drink, which made for stimulating conversation. Our hosts managed to squeeze in a visit to the souks, where we saw falcons being displayed and flying above us. For our anniversary we were recommended a restaurant at the very top floor of a skyscraper, where we saw nothing but twinkly lights. We could have been anywhere. But it turned out to be an intimate and emotional evening where we talked about what we wanted with the time we had left together. Eric was sorry he had spent so much time on his book *Fractured Times* and he was now going to stop, so we would spend more time together. A lovely thought, all good intentions, but totally naïve. He was a writer, and would no more be able to stop writing than a bird could stop nesting. And why should he? He was the one with little time left for living.

Chapter 25
Hospital Years

The title of this chapter doesn't necessarily refer to the amount of time we spent in hospitals, but is, rather, a metaphor for the constant struggle we faced in going out and about – it felt like preparing to go on the Kon-Tiki expedition each time. We would have everything ready: our tickets for the opera or concert, flowers for the hostess if going to a dinner, and so on. En route to our event he would often turn to me and say, 'I really don't feel too good,' and we would have to turn back. Some years back he had developed leukaemia, which was on the whole not troublesome, but it meant that his immune system could not cope with even the slightest temperature or bug. He was advised to go straight to the hospital if he began to feel unwell. Often this would result in unplanned trips to a (rather nice and quiet) cancer ward. We had our routine of going back and forth to the Royal Free. I used to say, like Laurel and Hardy, 'Another fine mess you have got us into.' We laughed and drank from our bottles of Volvic. Unfortunately after a while, this little cancer ward closed down and we had to endure going to A&E. More often than not, I would phone Julia, who would soon turn up with his favourite fruit sweets and an interesting story from the media world. Of course this cheered him up.

Eric was still mobile in these days, with a stick. He was not in serious pain and had all his marbles. He had problems with swallowing and this was the most depressing part of his condition. What he found so dispiriting was that he needed to eat, but it would take such a long time. He would often have prepared liquid formula, which contained the right substances, but he found them disgusting and like baby food. Keeping his weight up was the main struggle.

At home, I used to ponder the best way to pass the time and keep an old intellectual stimulated and happy. I learned it was best not to dwell on the specifics of medication, pill reminders and all the pragmatic health matters. My ploy was to ask questions like, 'If you could only take one book to an island, would it be Bernard Shaw?' or, 'Do you prefer Bellini or Schubert?' That would bring us back to the memory of a glorious Tuscan day at Benedetta Origo's house, when her cousin made the marvellous remark, 'Bellini was *our* Schubert.' This had always remained with us. The mind has to be taken away from the illness. The questions had to be light choices that could be easily made, rather than ones that demanded too much thinking. This time period also forced me to slow down and be fully present with him.

We were so close in our last chapter together. It was 24 September when I had to take him to the Royal Free for one of his routine blood transfusions. He was very comfortable with this procedure, which allowed him to read, and he would always be perkier and restored afterwards. Normally, I would come at around six to take him home.

But this time, I had a hunch and decided to pop in to see him at lunchtime. I found him worse than when he went in. A staff nurse then advised me, 'I really don't think you should take him home today. He's not well enough and he should spend the night here.' I stayed with him in an annexe to the ward.

The following morning his regular doctors did not appear as usual, and it was clear he was being moved to palliative care. The doctor said, 'We will keep him as comfortable as we can and we will see how we go day by day.' I phoned Andy and Julia and told them these were the last days. Then I phoned his favourite carer, Benny Fernandes, an Indian lady who loved both communism and Jesus. She shaved and cared for him in her way (the nurses had no time for that). He lived another six days and looked pretty good. He had some discomfort but no real pain – all that was taken care of. The grandchildren came, and I phoned some friends and organised the schedule as best I could. Luckily, one of his dearest friends, Leslie Bethell, was in London at that time. These visits did him good. He was lucid and pretty normal. On Andy's last visit, Eric asked, 'Do you think this is the end? Or will there be a final chapter?' to which Andy replied, 'Definitely one more chapter to go, Dad.'

The last evening, I felt that he had begun the process of dying. He was nearly deaf, so I had to get into his bed and talk right into his ear. I knew he didn't want to die, so I told him, 'Another fine mess you've got us into.' And he smiled. When I got out of his bed and stood at the end of it, he pointed at me, looked at me and repeated, 'You, you, you, you.' I knew he was trying to thank me for everything, and then he slept and that would be our final goodbye.

He died in the very early hours of the next morning, in his sleep, on 1 October 2012. The hospital phoned Julia around 4 a.m. and the three of us then went over. I have learned that one does not really expect the expected, and so we were, all three of us, in total shock.

Chapter 26
Death

The news of Eric's death instantly went viral all over the world. He was often the headlines on the main page, not tucked away in the obituary columns. Even *The Times* leader was about his death. One would think he had been the president of a major country. We bought all the papers, and the private condolence letters arrived at the same time. Home became a 24/7 international mail and newsroom. The phones never stopped ringing at all hours, time zones forgotten by those waking up to the news, and it was difficult to concentrate. It was overwhelming for me because of what was going on inside my head, which was gobbledygook. I seemed quite unable to grasp the fact that Eric was now not existing in the world at all any more, not anywhere, not for anyone. I felt I could have borne the cruelty better if he had gone far away, even left me for someone else, because this way of not existing in the world meant the world itself was now not a thing for me. It was like a form of delirium; I wondered if other bereaved people have had this disorienting experience. Quite paradoxically, I also felt relief. Only a week earlier I was making enquiries about a nearby nursing home, because I sensed the looming disability facing Eric. Soon he would be unable to stand or turn around on his own, however slowly. Our life as we knew it would be over. He would have to be lifted and need two carers during the day and also one at night. Now I didn't have to worry about those things any more, nor most importantly, worry about how Eric was feeling – that was all over. Eric's friend Nicholas Jacobs, from way back in Communist Party days and also our family friend, had recently surfaced again in our lives. He was alone now, and came around often, we called him our *Hausfreund*. With him came interesting talk, and cheer to our house and to our sad predicament. He liked having meals with us and we enjoyed that too. Actually, until the final weakening, before Eric was in hospital, we were still happily going out to the cinema, often the three of us, followed by a restaurant (usually Chinese) for a post-film discussion. Nick kindly came to all our funeral meetings, with his immeasurable knowledge of classical music, to help Andy, Julia and I. Eric had written his wishes for the funeral – which was to be held at Golders Green Crematorium – a long time beforehand and we kept about 80 per cent of them. Andy, a wizard on his mobile phone, found what we wanted in seconds, and Nick knew by heart the best recordings and with the best singers. I wanted the first orchestral bars of Bellini's 'Casta Diva' from the opera *Norma* to accompany the pallbearers. We were lucky that on the actual day, the number of bars matched exactly with their steps to the resting place of the coffin. Then came music by Beethoven, Mozart and, surprisingly to some, Offenbach and not surprisingly, instrumental jazz – 'Slow Grind' played by the Kenny Barron Trio. Of the many tributes and readings, the highlights were a tour de force eulogy by the historian Roy Foster and also moving memories spoken by Andy. In his written wishes, Eric had specified a non-religious funeral, and yet it was he himself who had previously (out of the blue) asked his friend Ira Katznelson if he would read the Kaddish at his funeral. Perhaps Eric was returning to a memory of when he was fourteen, remembering the advice and wish of his dying mother: that he must never do anything to suggest he was ashamed of being a Jew. When the time came, Ira made a flash visit from New York with his wife Debbie to say the Jewish prayer and then caught the 'red eye' back that same night. Eric had agreed with me that he wanted the melody of 'The Internationale' for the final piece and also exit music, and Andy's mobile searches had come up with a particularly fine French orchestral rendition, which was triumphant with tambourines instead of the usual solemnity. Many in the congregation sang the words out loud and heartily. The funeral ended on an uplifting note, which prevailed at the lunch served with much friendliness by staff at the nearby pub, the Bull and Bush. Andy and Julia came home with me, and some relations too. By six o'clock I was on my own and I knew the best thing for me was my reliable Beethoven therapy: a hot drink, a rug, a good armchair and more or less any Beethoven CD. This time I chose the Ninth Symphony because it begins chaotically and seemingly without a plan (as I found myself that day) but soon it would settle down, and if I had nodded off, the 'Ode to Joy' was sure to wake and revive me. It was in this way that I ended my saddest day.

Chapter 27
What Remains

Beginning with a death certificate, there is a huge amount of paperwork that comes as uninvited as death itself. Lawyers, the bank, the funeral parlour and the cemetery gravediggers – all have to be handled in turn. It is a busy period, unfortunately coinciding with the time needed for quiet reflection. Friends suggested I see a bereavement counsellor, and after deliberating, I decided I would try it. My counsellor was an intelligent and pleasant lady, and although the sessions didn't necessarily lift me out of my gloominess, having a space set aside each week meant there was dedicated time for thinking exclusively about Eric and 'us'. Where should I start? I decided to dwell on both our bad and good traits as individuals, which comforted me. I started with Eric. Although there was never a whiff of any dalliances on my part, he could be very possessive. I can understand this, knowing how much he suffered after his first wife left him for another man. I am convinced that at that time he would have blamed himself, although they were never a good couple and had great difficulties. Surely adding his culpabilities did not help him.

His experiences of childhood loss were such that I could never understand how it was that Eric was not more damaged or warped as a person. Nicholas Jacobs has a theory that if you experience good mothering in your first two years, you will cope with whatever life throws at you. But if you are deprived of this, then you are in trouble. I agree. Eric's mother thought the world of him from day one and their relationship was always close. In spite of his mother's death when he was only fourteen and having to work as an au pair, Eric knew about loving – relatives, friends, books, birds and American cars. Fortunately, he did overcome his breakdown after Muriel left him, and without any professional help. With pure strength of character, and his ambition to work and write like hell, he succeeded in conquering his unhappiness. It was really very impressive and admirable. Unfortunately there was no one to impress or to admire him; this was a very long and lonely stretch of time in his life. Many people, friends even, did not realise what an emotional man Eric was by nature. His relationship with Ticlia our cat was a familiar one – the less notice he took of her, the more attention she wanted. This went on for fourteen years. In the end, when she became very ill and could only drag her hind legs, we booked an appointment with the vet to have her put down. Eric said he had better come with me because I probably wouldn't manage the upset. The vet told Eric to hold Ticlia tight while he prepared the fatal injection. There was instant collapse. She did not suffer at all. Eric, however, had huge tears streaming down his face, 'I thought of Auschwitz,' he said. When the bill came he paid it twice by mistake.

A bad trait of mine was that I was mentally lazy. As Eric only took a few seconds to look things up in print and I was slow, he got into the habit of doing it all and that was unfair. I think he must have looked up the time of every train we took in fifty years. He did the heavy lifting of the household paperwork, the car, and all the utility contracts etc., though he did have secretaries to assist through his later years. I am ashamed now how much we all relied on Eric's knowledge. I would sometimes be lazy about the details of a news story and simply ask, 'Whose side are we on'? Officialdom is an alien language to me now. Serves me right. The one particular thing I regret above all else is preventing him from travelling to visit Isfahan in Iran. He was passionate about Oriental and Islamic art, and this was one of the most glorious places to see it. He had been thinking about it for years, but when the time came he was frail and I was struggling to keep his health up. I didn't want to witness it all unravelling. We had contacts there with Iranian scholars and would have been generously looked after, but I was nervous all the same. I had miscalculated badly – all the glories of Istfahan could be visited online, but still he minded terribly not going. He resented it for ever. I felt I had denied him his last supper and still feel rotten about it.

At times I noticed Eric and I had different degrees of loving. When Eric was proud of me, I think his love increased; when I published my recorder books, he was very excited that I had managed to do this. I suppose my love also increased at times, but for opposite reasons, like when he left his briefcase on the plane. I would think to myself, 'He's just a really ordinary Joe, but he's *my* ordinary Joe.' It seemed as though when I was clever he loved me most, and when he was stupid and silly I loved him most. Our love was an attraction of opposites. During my period of grieving, I also found solace in the writings of Rabindranath Tagore, recommended to me by our friend Amartya Sen. Tagore's words on death were profound – his concept of 'making friends with death' made such an impression on me. Another solace was my choir sessions, where we often sang from John Rutter's *Madrigals and Partsongs*. How happy I was singing John Wilbye's words, 'I hope when I am dead in Elysian plain to meet, and there with joy we'll love again.'

I did actually see Eric one last time. I know that sounds strange, but let me explain. Four months after his death, I was recovering from a hip replacement at the Royal Free Hospital, and was heavily sedated with morphine. Someone had turned on the TV, and there was Eric on the screen as clear as day, wearing one of his very smart suits, the kind he wore when meeting dignitaries; he looked marvellous. I was obviously having some kind of a hallucination, but I remember it vividly and can conjure it up now. He was looking directly at me and had a soft little smile.

Chapter 28
Eric's Legacy to Me

Of all the precious influences Eric left me, inherited friendships were the most important. They were aside from my beloved family and relatives, as well as musician friends. I call these my Team Eric: they were his friends, then became ours, and now they are mine, and I love to have them around. The Aschersons – Neal and Isobel, Leslie Bethell, the Fosters – Roy and Aisling, the Frayns – Claire and Michael, the Gotts – Richard and Vivien, Martin Jacques, Nicholas Jacobs, Jane Miller, Donald Sassoon, Marina Lewycka, Marina Warner, Graeme Segal, Joseph Rykwert, Gaia and Hugh Myddleton. Some are Eric's ex-students, many are mostly now in their sixties and seventies (creeping into their eighties), and many live in north London. The exceptions are Gaia, whom I knew before Eric did; Leslie Bethell, who lives in Rio de Janeiro but also teaches in London; Joseph, who is in his nineties (with all his marbles); Nicholas, whom Eric knew from Communist Party days; and Martin, whom we met together.

They all stayed loyal to me. They knew I had lived

with a human encyclopaedia for fifty years, and now I could consult with them instead to sort out my dilemmas. I hope I didn't exploit their kindness too much. It was at my request that many of these Team Eric friends obligingly prepared tributes and delivered wonderful words at the London memorial service for Eric. This was held at Senate House in April 2013, and Birkbeck pulled out all the stops to make it a splendid occasion. Roy Foster kindly hosted and Professors Roderick Floud, Frank Trentmann and Jean Seaton gave tremendous speeches. I also spoke a few words, recalling what a varied and privileged life I had being an academic's wife. Those were the days; we were very lucky and the two of us made a good fist of it. Today I get the impression academic life is much harsher, probably for financial reasons.

I had decided already that I didn't want to stay in our house in Nassington Road any more. I wanted to sell it. It would make the final exodus complete. The children had flown, Ticlia had died and now Eric was gone too. 'Knock knock.' 'Who's there? 'Only Marlene,' and her life within it had disappeared. The house was too big for me on my own. Mainly, the thought of living there without Eric would be like rubbing salt in the wound every day. Leaving my lovely neighbours would be very sad. Rena, Marion and Rob and co., Chris and Dominique Moore, Nick and Ghislaine, the Southgates next door, Berwyn, Charlotte, Jim, and the girls. One evening a letter slid under my door from a couple who lived down Parliament Hill, asking me would I please not sell the house until they'd seen it as they had their heart set on it. They were extremely nice people who still invite me to visit 'my' garden from time to time. Over in Belsize Park, I came across a handsome block of flats and went straight to the estate agent to make enquiries. I was told there was a flat for sale on the first floor, but the owners were in Australia. I would have to wait to see inside until they returned. Very tantalising. I waited two months, then went to inspect with Anna Rosa and Federica Frishman. We all liked the flat immensely, especially the abundance of natural light, even though there were one or two quite radical changes that would have to be made. Despite this, I knew it was right for me; just like with a fella, one knows immediately. No matter what issue, I still thought about what Eric's opinion would be, and when it came to the new flat, I think he would have approved. Being an architect, Federica generously offered her help, and her experienced builder was available, which was indispensable, considering I had last renovated and refurbished a house forty long years ago, and that was before the internet. Now, alas all of the ordering of fittings and furnishings had to be dealt with online. Luckily it suited Federica, who was a marvellous organiser, never without her tape measure to hand. If there was a problem, she would have it sorted before you could say 'Jack Robinson'. With the changes I intended to make, I would have a large music room able to accommodate a dozen recorder players

I had to borrow the money urgently and pay the deposit in order to secure the flat; I was already beginning to plunge into huge decisions like this on my own. It was a tense race, but I made it in time because my unflappable son-in-law Alaric helped me with the transaction of the money. In this new home I altered my way of hospitality, no longer holding dinner parties, since I felt the absence of Eric's partnership in hosting. Always observant and inclusive,

Eric had been the main conversationalist, though I grew into discussing world affairs without him. Certainly I had become more daring, developing a new self-confidence to express my opinions. Indeed, the confidence that developed over fifty years in a loving marriage served me well just when I needed it. For entertaining, I've found Sunday lunchtime to be the most relaxed part of the week for guests. Those tending to their gardens or allotments – like the Fosters – can come and go in their wellies. Usually I invite some of the 'Team', as well as integrating new faces. I still prefer, when possible, one conversation for us all around the table, and refer to the meal as brunch, to indicate they should not expect a three-course meal with a duck in the middle. These are jolly occasions. Nicholas is perhaps the most loyal guest and usually arrives earlier in order to help with the drinks. I call him the barista. Nick is a retired publisher who translates, writes book reviews and teaches German literature to adults at U3A. I did exploit him regarding help with the academic mail, which has now finally dwindled. I knew he could keep secrets, and he helped me with my dilemmas in assisting Richard Evans, who was writing a biography of Eric. It took seven years and brought our friendship closer. Luckily for me, Nick is a total culture vulture. He first introduced me to concert performances of early opera and subscribed to those conducted by Ian Page, the artistic director of Classical Opera and the Mozartists. They perform in all the London venues: Cadogan Hall, Royal Festival Hall, Wigmore Hall and St John's Smith Square. I find opera performed in this intimate way intensely moving. Above all, Nick plied me with books. He was amazed I had not read *Madame Bovary* – so I did and it provided discussion for weeks. Also my first Goethe, which I adored: *The Sorrows of Young Werther*. As soon as I finished it I began at the beginning again. I thought his writing both prosaic and glorious. Then came the most precious of books, *Clean Young Englishman*, a short autobiography by John Gale, a sensitive and superb prose writer. Books became a lifeline for me. It is very common for new widows to have accidents, and I was no exception. I broke my right ankle in a car crash, then fractured my right wrist in a fall and sprained my left hand at the same time. This often left me stationary at home with a carer.

Unfortunately in life, one never knows what is around the corner; while out shopping one Saturday morning, my phone began to ring – it was Walter's eldest daughter Habie to tell me my brother Walter had died. I dropped everything and put the supermarket in disarray. Again, I was in a state of disbelief. We'd been close ever since our Vienna days and into our adulthood. Because of our shared childhood, he helped, in fact checking the earlier parts of this memoir. Walter was very popular in his family, including with all the children and grandchildren. He made time for everyone, no matter the issue. If funerals are supposed to console, then Walter's provided the most consolation there could be. Aside from his many friends, all the nieces, nephews, children and grandchildren went to such lengths and effort with their songs and music, clever and funny speeches – his son Ben had everyone in tears. Because Walter had begun to develop Alzheimer's, there was also a sense of relief for anyone who really loved him.

Apart from my friends, it is of course my children who really sustain me. They are part of me, and so are their families. 'Next of kin' are three powerful words. Both my children are now absorbed in their various work projects. Julia, a published author, writes and lectures about technology and human connections, and also runs an events and consulting business. Andy is an internet entrepreneur and digital adviser working with a number of start-up ventures and other businesses; he also writes and performs music with his singer/songwriter wife Kate. Despite their hard work and success in their careers, Andy and Julia and their spouses are very good parents. They manage to raise their children so well in these difficult times, with huge dedication and thought. We all stay close. Julia and Andy usually pop in on the weekend. We have a family arrangement to meet on the first Sunday of the month, when both families come around to my place for bagels, cream cheese, smoked salmon, salami and much more. The schedule sometimes has to move when Julia or Andy is travelling for work, but the grandchildren (now all teenagers) like it very much and we all make an effort to keep up the tradition. Luckily, Highgate Cemetery is nearby for us all to visit Eric's grave, which is made of fine Kirkby grey slate from Cumbria, with incisive lettering carved by Annet Stirling. Depending on how you approach the grave (and perhaps your political beliefs) it is situated either a little to the right or a little to the left of Karl Marx.

So there is life after Eric. I still feel his presence, and talk to him – he always was a good listener. In whimsical moments, I daydream about meeting him in Buenos Aires after all.

Acknowledgements

M y thanks especially go to Claire Tomalin for agree-
ing to do an introduction and for writing such a
thoughtful and flattering piece; Jane Miller for being the
first friend to read a draft of this book in its raw initial
stage; to both my children, Andy and Julia, who helped jog
my memory and encouraged me all along the way; Julia for
putting me in contact with Sarah and Kate Beal at Muswell
Press, who accepted my book and were so warm and kind;
helpful friends Leslie Bethell, Martin Jacques, Donald
Sassoon, Nick Jacobs and Anna Rosa Villari; Bruce Hunter
and Margaret Bluman for their advice; Joan Martínez Alier
for helping me through the Agrarian Reform in Peru;
Divya Osbon for stepping in during a sticky situation; my
assistant Holly Parmley, a writer and artist, who initially
came to assist me on the computer and typing, but as our
friendship grew, her role changed to help me with the
writing of this book, which took us two years to finish.

Photo Credits

All photos from the Hobsbawm family archive with the exception of :

Marlene in Capri at the Arco Naturale. Photo by Mariella de Sarzana

Eric in Marlene's Paddington Street flat during their early dating. Photo by Marlene

Eric bonding with our first born Andy. Photo by Marlene

Roman, Anoushka, Max, Rachael and Wolfie. Photo by Rachael Campbell

Marlene and Eric. Photo by Enzo Crea